JENNIFER SCHELL

The Butcher, The Baker, The Wine & Cheese Maker

AN OKANAGAN COOKBOOK

LIBRARY AND ARCHIVES CANADA CATALOGUING IN PUBLICATION

The Butcher, The Baker, The Wine & Cheese Maker, An Okanagan Cookbook
Jennifer Schell
ISBN 978-0-9917498-0-5
A catalogue record for this publication is available from the
National Library of Canada.

Publisher/Editor: An Okanagan Cookbook
Photography: Jennifer Schell (with contributions from Spatula Media +
Communications)
Designer: Kirk Myltoft, Gecko Design & Advertising

www.anokanagancookbook.com

Printed in Canada

L-R (standing) Jörg Hoffmeister (Owner/Chef/Chocolatier, Dolci Deli & Catering), Helen Kennedy (Beekeeper/Owner, Arlo's Honey), Jeff Martin (Winemaker/Owner La Frenz Winery), Grant Stanley (Winemaker, Quails' Gate Winery), Rod Butters (Chef/Owner RauDZ Regional Table), Monika Walker (Baker/Owner, Okanagan Grocery - Artisan Breads), Gabe Cipes (Farmer/Forager Summerhill Pyramid Winery), Gene Covert (Farmer/Owner Covert Farms) Richard Yntema (Owner/Butcher/Farmer North Okanagan Game Meats).
L-R (seated) Dana Ewart (Chef/Owner Joy Road Catering), Jennifer Schell (Editor/Cookbook Author), Ofri Barmor (Owner/Cheesemaker Carmelis Goat Cheese Artisans) and Claude (Rooster Extraordinaire).

Check out our website www.anokanagancookbook.com for more recipes and an Okanagan directory including how to find the people, farms, restaurants and businesses in this book.

BON APPÉTIT

"This cookbook is a love letter to all those who have created, grown and nurtured our special valley on this earth."

Jennifer Schell

Photo: Jonathan Schell

I was farm raised on this beautiful Okanagan soil. Proud of my family's farming history with generations of farmers on both sides, I was instilled with a deep respect for the good earth and for those who tend it.

My 95-year-old Grandma Katherine Weisbeck recounts stories of me hopping through the orchard, pigtails flying, with a fistful of wild violets en route for a visit. I was so fortunate to grow up with grandparents living on farms on either side of us. She was a fabulous baker and I would love to take my seat – on a large flour tin stacked onto a chair - and watch her bake. She had eight children to cook for and her garden and kitchen production were a marvel to observe.

Oma and Opa Schell lived on the other side of our farmhouse until they retired. Their kitchen was another delicious culinary destination for me as a child. Oma's chicken noodle soup remains the best I have ever had. Chock-full of long, homemade egg noodles and rich farm chicken broth – it is a wonderful sensory memory. Soup and homemade sweet milk buns were followed by a slice of her legendary Sugar Kuchen (a German-Russian dessert)- unfortunately, many have tried but none seem to be able to completely replicate the texture of hers. My palate was honed on homemade, homegrown, made-from-scratch cuisine – and the bar was set high.

My Dad, John Schell, immigrated to Canada in 1950 at the age of eight from Germany with his family and a transport bill of $2,000 in their pockets. Sponsored by a distant relative, who owned a restaurant called the Schell Grill on Bernard Avenue, the family first worked for him to pay off their debt before getting numerous jobs around town. A family of five, they worked together – first to survive and eventually to make a good living. After only four years, in the fall of 1954, through hard work and focus, they were able to purchase their own orchard in East Kelowna – an extraordinary feat.

The harvest time in the 1950's was a crucial period for my family and entailed much more than a fruit harvest. Dad says after they got the fruit off the trees and to the packing house and cannery, it was time to press the grapes for wine (using my Opa's handmade grape press), get the potatoes and hearty vegetables into cellar storage and preserve the fruits and vegetables. Once those chores were complete, when the weather cooled in November, they would butcher pigs and make sausage. Today, we call it sustainability – they called it survival. Then it was time for a celebration dinner. Usually a pig roast, the wine flowed, the table was laden with their hard earned bounty and they would share the feast with friends and family and raise their glasses to life.

It is amazing to imagine that their family was almost completely self-sufficient – from produce to meat to dairy products to wine to soap. Opa's deep respect for his land, knowledge of how to grow food, raise food and create from the earth is the foundation of our food and wine culture here. This life giving soil gave them everything they needed to survive and so it remains for us.

This cookbook is a love letter to all those who have created, grown and nurtured our special valley on this earth. They are a delightful confluence of old and new world, blending their international influence and flavours with our local bounty, establishing a cuisine that is distinctly Okanagan. Through their recipes and stories, I am pleased to introduce you to these gifted people who bring this local food to your table every day.

Thank you, to the farmers, orchardists, winemakers, artisans, chefs, butchers, bakers and wine and cheese makers for your passion and commitment to making our world a more delicious, healthful place to be and for taking the time to share your stories with me. Thank you for teaching us your old world sustainability practices, reminding us to treasure the good earth we have been blessed with, and setting the table for the generations who will follow.

Jennifer Schell

"I lift my glass to all our gifted chefs and winemakers, and to all others who have contributed to the growth of the local dining experience and to all who will do so in the future, including you, the reader."

Harry McWatters

Thanks so very much to Jennifer Schell for allowing me the privilege of writing this foreword. She has assembled an amazing array of recipes and wine pairings, and embodies the Okanagan Valley spirit of eating local, drinking local, and being local. This book celebrates our unique cuisine, and, just as wine is a reflection of its terroir, so are the fruits, vegetables, meats and cheeses of this bountiful region.

British Columbia's Okanagan Valley has long been recognized as a major Canadian "fruit basket," providing the rest of Canada with a wide variety of fruits, including cherries, peaches, apples and table grapes. I can well remember, as a young boy in Toronto, finding a shiny, pristine British Columbia extra-large, extra-fancy Red Delicious apple that became simply known as our "Christmas apples."

Having been in the wine business since 1968, I can attest to the fact that, contrary to popular belief, we had some good wines here in the Okanagan, and some interesting places to dine. However, they were few and far between, and merely a reflection of the consumer demands of the day.

The late 80's brought in the North American Free Trade Agreement, and with it, radical changes to the landscape for British Columbia wines and vineyards. At that time there were only 14 wineries and approximately 3,400 acres of vines. In 1989 we saw the pull out of all but about 1,000 acres of grapes, removing virtually all of the Labrusca varietals (like Concord) and most of the hybrids (like Marechal Foch, Chelois, Verdelet and DeChaunac), leaving primarily vitis vinifera (the true European wine grape varieties, like Riesling, Chardonnay, Gewürztraminer, Merlot, Pinot Noir and Cabernet Sauvignon, to name just a few) to establish a new foundation for the future of the wine industry. This was followed by the launch of the Vintners' Quality Alliance (VQA) in 1990. I may be slightly biased, but I believe that was the beginning of an era for the grape and the wine industry as well as the culinary environment in our area. I personally believe that without the introduction of VQA, we would likely not have a wine industry in British Columbia today, and most certainly not the thriving enterprise as we know it. As this industry found its legs, it attracted new wineries, new winemakers and new investments. This fresh era, in my opinion, was the catalyst for growth, fostering novel and exciting dining opportunities as the wine industry grew and garnered international acclaim by winning prestigious awards such as "Best of Variety", "Best of Class" and "Best of Show" at some of the most prominent wine competitions held throughout Europe and North America. This has spurred demand for broader, diverse dining experiences, focusing on local, sustainable agriculture.

Today our region can boast more than 200 wineries and several micro breweries and craft distilleries with great diversity in variety and style, all giving the consumer an array of choices to pair with the myriad culinary experiences offered at many of the fine restaurants and farmers' markets throughout the valley.

Locals and visitors alike welcome the return each spring of the outdoor markets, with their colourful displays of seasonal produce, artisan breads and baked goods, flowers, honey, maple syrup, and the like, interspersed with stands selling works by local artists, hand-crafted jewelry, cedar furniture, food carts and a wide variety of other goods. Who can resist the fresh cinnamon buns, paired with an aromatic cup of coffee to sustain you while you shop for tonight's dinner? Later in the day, there are so many things to discover in the towns and on the back roads of the Okanagan. In addition to the local wineries, restaurants and cafes, you will find local cheese producers, jam makers, artists' workshops and roadside fruit stands.

Wineries offer a diverse variety of food pairing events, from upscale European cuisine to outdoor pig roasts, there is always something going on in the valley. Not only can you eat and drink, you can soak up the lake views and relax on a deck in the sun while you enjoy your glass of wine and fresh, local meal. Festivals go on throughout the year, with spring, summer and fall wine festivals, interspersed with hundreds of food and wine events.

Future chefs, winemakers and producers will be inspired by the mouthwatering dishes contained in the pages of this book. They represent the future evolution of the Okanagan Valley and will play an important role in building its reputation as one of the great culinary regions of Canada. We hope that what you read here will also help to enhance your creativity and desire to experiment with the abundance of fantastic local ingredients and wines which we are blessed to have in this special corner of the world.

I lift my glass to all our gifted chefs and winemakers, and to all others who have contributed to the growth of the local dining experience and to all who will do so in the future, including you, the reader.

Cheers!

Harry McWatters

Harry McWatters Collection

We currently have two of our releases available from the McWatters Collection. The Meritage is 44% Cabernet Sauvignon, 32% Merlot and 24% Cabernet Franc. I describe this wine as being big, elegant, with soft tannins, well-balanced fruit and oak characteristics with blackberry and cassis overtones. It will complement grilled meats, roasts, and rich tomato pastas, and is best when shared with friends (new and old). The McWatters Collection Chardonnay is vinified from 100% Chardonnay grapes, rich and elegant, with well-balanced fruit and oak characteristics with notes of pineapple, tropical fruit, hints of honey, lemon zest and buttered toast. This opulent Chardonnay has a lingering dry finish.

Both of these wines were 100% grown in my Sundial Vineyard, located on the Black Sage Bench in Oliver. I personally guarantee every bottle of wine that bears my name. You will find my personal email address on the back label.

Community… A simple word that means so much. For me, this cookbook is all about community. Whether you are a chef, a cheesemaker, a fishmonger, raising free-range chickens, making world-class wines or an inspired home cook, we are all part of the community of food. We share a love and a passion for food and this is what holds our community together.

This cookbook is more than just filled with delicious recipes, it shares the stories of our relationships, the seasonality of our menus and how we celebrate food here in the Okanagan.

When I first arrived in the Okanagan Valley, I felt a little like a food pioneer. There were few of us in the food community and were really foraging our own way. Slowly, we met like-minded farmers and other artisans that shared our philosophy of 'Support Local, Buy Local, Eat & Drink Local'. The idea of using local ingredients on our restaurant menus began to pollinate up and down the valley with renowned chefs discovering the Okanagan and setting down roots. Our local cuisine was a natural pairing for the award winning world class wines that were being produced in the valley. Their wines, the farmers amazing produce and our menus were slowly establishing the Okanagan as a culinary destination. There is no more exciting region to be cooking in right now.

Sharing our passion and love of food comes naturally to us and we encourage our neighbourhood to appreciate and celebrate their food with events like the Garlic Festival, Salmon Festival, Feast of Fields, and to shop our burgeoning local farmers markets.

In my kitchen at the restaurant, I want my young cooks to understand the food they are preparing so we often take field trips out of the kitchen and to the farm where they will see a wild boar, make cheese, or pick bushels of tomatoes. The experience connects everyone to the land, to the food and equally important, to the person who is growing or raising this product for our menu.

As Past President and Chairman of the Okanagan Chefs Association, I'm very proud of our members and how we've become one of the fastest growing, most active associations in the country. Our success is based on the idea of community. We come together to share ideas, share our culinary war stories and to share the success of our efforts by helping the less fortunate of our community through many fundraising initiatives. I often refer to the Okanagan Valley as 'the ultimate chefs playground'. I believe in what we in the valley have to offer and how as chefs working with our farmers, artisans, and winemakers, we can truly promote the Okanagan on the world stage.

Congratulations to Jennifer for bringing our food community together within these pages.

Chef Rod Butters, WCC
Chef/Owner RauDZ Regional Table, Kelowna BC
Inductee, BC Restaurant Hall of Fame 2007,
Proud member of the Okanagan Food Community
"When you cook with passion, you feed the soul"

"I believe in what we in the valley have to offer and how as chefs working with our farmers, artisans, and winemakers, we can truly promote the Okanagan on the world stage."

Chef Rod Butters

FarmGate Foundation

A portion of proceeds from the sales of The Butcher, The Baker, The Wine & Cheese Maker – An Okanagan Cookbook will be donated to the newly created FarmGate Foundation. These funds will be the seed money to launch this latest initiative in cooperation with the Okanagan Chefs Association. The FarmGate Foundation is focused towards feeding our future with community gardens, an initiative for growing food for donation to needy organizations, educational opportunities, cooking demonstrations and building the relationships of the farmers, the community and the land.

The FarmGate Foundation will be shepherded by eating local advocates, OCA Past Presidents and Chefs Rod Butters and Geoffrey Couper along with An Okanagan Cookbook author Jennifer Schell.

"Copper Shovel"
Kelowna Metal Artist
Amber Denison

Starters

Baby Beet & Fromage Frais Salad, Fresh Raspberry Vinaigrette, Micro-Lettuces

Chef: Roger Sleiman, Old Vines Restaurant, Quails' Gate Estate Winery, West Kelowna
Farmer: Tony Cetinski, Suncatcher Farm, Kelowna
Winemaker: Quails' Gate Estate Winery, West Kelowna

For many, summer is a favourite season to cook. Dishes can be simple. The rich intensity of the fresh picked fruits, vegetables and herbs on hand do not require much labour. Salads are a mouthwatering treat, chock full of lettuces, cucumbers, berries, tomatoes, radishes, carrots – they hardly need a dressing at all. If ever one was to become a vegetarian, this is the time.

Beautiful fresh cheese served on a salad of colourful beets spiked with local raspberries will ignite your midsummer night's meal. Baby beets in season are tender and sweet and available at the farmers' markets from July through to October. They are great to pickle for a winter treat; make sure to wear plastic gloves when peeling them or you will have pretty pink hands to match the dish.

Sigh, there is nothing like a midsummer Okanagan night.

Serves 4

1.5 lbs (680gr) of assorted baby beets such as chiogga, golden & red
1 cup fromage frais (aka fromage blanc) *may substitute buffalo mozzarella, or goat cheese
salt & pepper
zest of 1 lemon (preferably organic)
micro lettuce or soft herbs such as chervil or Italian parsley

Raspberry Vinaigrette
1 cup raspberries
250 ml raspberry vinegar (local suggestion: Vinegar Works, Summerland)
4 tbsp honey
¼ tsp dry mustard
750 ml olive oil

Blend raspberries and vinegar then strain through a fine sieve. Add honey, salt and mustard powder. While whisking, slowly add the oil. Season with salt and pepper to taste.

In a large pot, cover beets with water and simmer until tender, strain. Using a cloth rub the skin, it should easily come off. Cut in half and set aside to cool.

Mix fromage frais with the lemon zest and season with salt to taste.

In two separate bowls, one for the red beets and the other for the gold and chiogga, lightly toss with vinaigrette. Season with salt and pepper. Colorfully arrange beets on large dish. Drizzle with more raspberry vinaigrette.

Spoon some fromage frais on top and arrange the soft herbs.

Chef Roger Sleiman (L) and Farmer Tony Cetinski

THE CHEF

Roger Sleiman, Old Vines Restaurant, Quails' Gate Estate Winery, West Kelowna

Chef Roger Sleiman was raised in Beirut, Lebanon and immigrated to Canada at the young age of 10. He was raised on simple Lebanese and Mediterranean fare, rural cuisine based on the simple ingredients of olive oil, lemon and garlic.

Chef Sleiman graduated top of his class during his culinary education at the Vancouver Community College, then went on to stints at Café Henry Burger in Ottawa, La Rua Restaurante and Val D'Isere Restaurant in Whistler. Quails' Gate Estate Winery welcomed Roger as Winery Chef in 2006, when the lure of the beautiful Okanagan Lake and family lifestyle drew him to the valley. Since that time Chef Sleiman has refocused the culinary program at Old Vines Restaurant with his basic cooking principles of keeping it simple, fresh, and staying true to the ingredients.

In His Own Words

"The Okanagan is absolute heaven for a chef. The local bounty is second to none. The local chef's community work together and helps each other on a regular basis... you don't see that very often in other cities.

Okanagan cuisine to me is a commitment to using seasonal product from the surrounding area and pairing it with our local wines. In the Okanagan, fresh produce is as important on the plate as the protein. It defines Okanagan cuisine. The agricultural heritage of the Okanagan is vital whenever you think of Okanagan cuisine. Adding to this are the ever-growing meat and dairy producers which now are able to supply chefs on a consistent basis.

The connection with my producers is a very enjoyable part of my job. We have become friends and experience the joys of harvest every year. Without them there would not be "Okanagan cuisine" and Old Vines Restaurant would not be what it is. From the farmer to the meat and fish supplier they are integral to our local industry."

THE FARMERS

Tony and Nancy Cetinski, Suncatcher Farm, Kelowna

"The greatest fine art of the future will be the making of a comfortable living from a small piece of land."
– Abraham Lincoln

In his own words:
"We bought our farm in 2001, with rose-coloured glasses firmly in place. I had never farmed a day in my life, but had always thought it would be a great lifestyle. Our farm is part of the oldest farmstead in Kelowna. The original owner was Eli Lequime; he bought a 160-acre parcel in 1885. To put that into context, our copy of the original deed was signed on behalf of Queen Victoria. He had three sons, Bernard, Lawrence and Leon. We grow Canada Certified Organic mixed vegetables on about five acres. It is light work - when it's light, I work (wink). Organic is just a simpler, more natural way to produce food. I prefer to think of my fields as a pantry, not a war zone.

I think that people are looking for more value in their food choices. I like to say that when we started, people were often looking for the cheapest food they could find, but are now looking for the best food they can afford. Large retailers certainly have their place, but people are more aware of the difference fresh makes. I would like to see more awareness of the importance of eating seasonally appropriate food, i.e. fresh peaches should not be expected in Kelowna in January.

Our relationship with local chefs is critical to our farm's future. They truly value our product and really understand what we do."

THE WINERY

Quails' Gate Estate Winery, West Kelowna

The Stewart Family are pioneers in the Okanagan farming industry. Arriving in Kelowna in 1908, Richard Stewart Sr. founded one of the valley's most successful nursery businesses. Fifty years later his son Dick Stewart decided to plant grapes and in 1989, the Stewart family founded Quails' Gate Winery.

In 1956 Dick (Richard) Stewart purchased the Quails' Gate Estate land on the west side of Kelowna. The first vines were planted in 1961 and today the family farms over 180 acres of vineyards in the valley. Dick's son, Tony Stewart, now is in charge of the winery operations.

Quails' Gate offers soaring views of Okanagan Lake as well as rich Okanagan history on the property. It has always been a mandate for the Stewart family to help preserve the heritage in the valley.

Winemaker Grant Stanley (right) is meticulous with his grape production and winemaking techniques. All grapes are hand picked and immediately de-stemmed to capture the fresh fruit character of his wines. With this in mind, you will note his wines are extremely aromatic, very fruit forward and well-balanced.

PAIRING

2011 Quails' Gate Rosé:

Pale pink with beautiful aromas of pink grapefruit, berries with a hint of pepper – this juicy Rosé is a perfect summer sipper and pairs well with food.

Baby Iceberg Lettuce w/ Blue Cheese Dressing

Chef: Paul Cecconi, Local Lounge • Grille, Summerland
Farmer: Tyler Harlton Farms, Summerland
Winemaker: Tyler Harlton Wines, Summerland

This gorgeous salad is a favorite on Local's menu. Plain old iceberg lettuce topped with these two rich and flavourful dressings is transformed into something elegant and absolutely delicious. There are so many different layers of flavour dancing on the palate with each bite – it's easy to see why this salad is a top seller.

Blue Cheese Dressing:
1/2 cup blue cheese, crumbled (local suggestion: Poplar Grove Tiger Blue)
3/4 cup sour cream
3/4 cup mayonnaise
1/4 cup buttermilk
1/2 tbsp coarse black pepper
1/2 tbsp local sherry vinegar

Combine all ingredients in Kitchen Aid and mix on medium speed for 3 minutes.

Mixed Mushroom-Okanagan Cherry Vinaigrette:
1 lb mixed mushrooms sliced (Shimeji, King Oyster, Shitake)
1/2 cup dried Okanagan cherries
2 slices bacon, julienned
2 shallots, sliced into rings
1 tbsp garlic, minced
3/4 cup rice vinegar
2 tbsp extra virgin olive oil
sea salt/cracked black pepper, to taste

Sauté the mushrooms in the olive oil in a med-high heat pan until soft. Add bacon, cherries and shallots and cook until bacon begins to crisp up. Deglaze the pan with rice vinegar and season to taste.

Assembly:
Cut iceberg into 6 wedges and place on dish and dress each wedge with the blue cheese dressing then dress each wedge with the warm mushroom dressing.
Enjoy!

17

The Chef

Chef Paul Cecconi, Local Lounge • Grille, Summerland

Inspired by his mother and grandmother's Tuscan cooking, Paul enrolled and graduated from Vancouver Community College Culinary Arts Program. After travelling and working for the Four Seasons Hotel in both Vancouver and Australia, he accepted the position of Executive Chef at The Harvest Golf Club in Kelowna. In 2009 he became Executive Chef at Local Lounge • Grille.

In his own words:
"I support organic/non organic as long as they are farming in an eco-friendly manner. I find my suppliers through word of mouth and from exploring the Okanagan. The relationship between chef and supplier is very important, as I am able to work with the grower to plan what they may grow for the upcoming season.
(To me) Okanagan cuisine is food that moves with the growing season, emphasis on wine and food pairings….keeping it fresh and local."

L-R: Mini Chef Simon Cecconi, Chef Paul Cecconi and Tyler Harlton

THE FARMER/WINEMAKER

Tyler Harlton, Tyler Harlton Farms - Summerland

Tyler Harlton is an organic grower and winemaker in Summerland making wines under his own name. A Saskatchewan boy, Tyler arrived in the Okanagan five years ago and met Winemaker William Adams who introduced him to winemaking. "When I received my licence last fall for the facility in Summerland I approached William and told him the plan: put our money into getting the best grapes and put our effort into making the best wine." Tyler also leases a piece of land in Summerland that he has transformed into an organic garden. Growing for Chefs like Paul Cecconi, at Local Lounge • Grille, Tyler also hosts a local farmers market on the property to purvey his wholesome produce to neighbours.

In his own words:
"The Okanagan is the closest thing Canada has to the Mediterranean. The summer is hot and dry, and the winters are mild, conditions that are attractive to a grower. On a personal note, the summers remind me of Saskatchewan, where the sun, the wind, and the rain are inescapable forces that fix you to the land. Organic farming requires the farmer to take notice of nature's complexity. It's inspiring to play a role in this web. Farming will not interest a future generation until small farmers are properly compensated. I'd like to see a future where small farmers figure out how to achieve this through their own means.

The local cuisine is unique because there's a vivid palette of food and wine to take advantage of. It's unique to me because as a farmer I love the rhythm of the crops as they come in and out of season."

PAIRING

Tyler Harlton Pinot Gris/Viognier

Fresh and floral, this wine pairs wonderfully with food. With notes of Okanagan stone fruit on the nose, the palate is crisp and mouthwatering with hints of lemon.

Rosé Wine Jelly
Ingredients: Sugar, Covert Farms Family Estate
Rose Wine, Lemon juice (water, concentrated
lemon juice, sodium sulfite,
sodium benzoate), Liquid pectin

Rosé Wine Jelly
This pretty and tasty wine jelly would also be divine served
with cheese.

Ingredients:
1 bottle Rosé wine
2 cups cane sugar
1 cup organic honey
6 oz liquid pectin

1. Pour 1 bottle of Rosé wine, cane sugar, and honey into
a double boiler and heat until dissolved and uniform.
The slower you heat the more wine will remain. Remove
from heat and allow to cool to room temperature.
2. Stir in pectin, and pour into desired container and
allow to cool in refrigerator to set.
3. Jelly can be poured into sterilized jars and sealed with
wax to be stored for up to 4 months.
(Be aware the alcohol will vaporize when rapidly heated.
Do not inhale deeply. If using a gas stove the wine may
ignite if flame is present under high heat.)

BRAWN TERRINE & ROSÉ WINE JELLY

CHEF: DEREK UHLEMANN, COVERT FARMS, OLIVER
FARMER: GENE COVERT, COVERT FARMS, OLIVER
WINEMAKER: COVERT FARMS FAMILY ESTATE WINERY, OLIVER

Terrines are gorgeous. From the rustic to the refined, the terrine explains much about the creator chef's tastes and terroir. Like a paté, a terrine is the vessel within which a forced meat (or vegetable) loaf is created. Very French, and sometimes challenging to create, a good terrine never fails to thrill.
Chef Derek has created this mouthwatering terrine focusing on the flavours from Covert Farms –vegetables and wine – which will create a flavour unique to the Covert land. Derek describes this as "a true winter starter, with winter hearty ingredients." I love the Rosé wine jelly as an accoutrement; it adds a touch of lightness with flavours of summer.

Brawn Terrine
Ingredients:
1 pig's head cleaned and washed (local suggestion: North Okanagan Game Meats)
8 litres water approximately
4 cups coarse salt (or 1 cup per litre as needed; refer to egg method below)
2 cups cane sugar (or 1/2 cup cane sugar for every litre water)
1 egg
2 organic Walla Walla onions, rough chopped
4 ribs organic fennel bulb, rough chopped
1 bulb organic garlic, peeled into cloves
8 bay leaves
6 cloves
12 whole peppercorns
1 bottle of Pinot Blanc (local suggestion: Covert Farms Family Estate Pinot Blanc)
1 bunch organic thyme tied with string
6 oz organic flat leaf parsley finely chopped
finely chopped organic fennel sprigs from one fennel bulb

Place the water in a pot and add the salt and sugar. Bring to a low boil. When the salt is completely dissolved remove the pot from the heat and add the egg in its shell. If the egg floats your brine is perfect! If your egg sinks and does not come back up, add more salt. Repeat until the egg floats. Let the brine cool and pour into a non-reactive storage container.
Wash the pig head in cold water and scrub thoroughly. If the head is hairy, use a kitchen torch to remove the bristles and whiskers.
Place the pig head in the non-reactive container, and cover with brine to submerge. Weigh the head down with a plate or a large glass jar filled with water and refrigerate overnight.
Remove the pig head in the morning and rinse well. Throw away the brine as you do not need it.
Place the pig head in a large stockpot and cover with water, add the 1/2 bottle of Pinot Blanc wine, Walla Walla onions, fennel, garlic cloves, bay leaves, cloves,

peppercorns, and thyme bundle. Bring the liquid to a boil and then immediately reduce the heat and simmer for 4-6 hours or until the jaw detaches. While you are simmering, skim off any grey foam that gathers on the top of the liquid and discard. The more you discard impurities, the clearer your gel will be. Do not stir or agitate the stock while it is cooking to avoid cloudiness.
When the meat is tender and falling off the bone, remove the meat from the stock, and set aside to cool. Ready a fine mesh strainer and a smaller stock pot to collect the stock. Line the strainer with cheesecloth or a clean kitchen cloth and strain the stock into your new smaller stock pot. Return the stock to the stove and on low heat, reduce the liquid by one half. Taste for salt and adjust allow to cool slightly.
Drink a glass of the Pinot Blanc to prepare for peeling the tongue. Remove the tongue from the head and peel the outer skin off. It should peel easily. Remove the remaining meat from the head and chop or pull it apart to form a small dice. Chop everything - the ears, soft pallet and all the bits and pieces. The texture of the terrine is what makes it so tasty.
Gather a terrine mold or a bread pan and line with plastic wrap allowing enough overhand so you have handles to remove your terrine when it has set. Mix all your meat in a bowl and combine in the mold, pressing down firmly. Pour stock over the meat until it covers the meat entirely. If you don't have a terrine mold, soup bowls will also work well and can allow you to freeze them individually for later use.
Layer your finely chopped parsley and fennel over the liquid and wrap tightly making sure everything is covered and neat. Make sure your layer of herbs is ample and spread evenly. Refrigerate overnight.
Unmold your cold terrine by grabbing your plastic handles and inverting it onto a plate or cutting board. Remove plastic slice and serve. Pour your final glass of Pinot Blanc.
Assemble your Brawn Terrine with Rosé Wine Jelly and organic sourdough loaf and enjoy!

Gene Covert (L)
with Derek Uhlemann

THE CHEF

Derek Uhlemann, Covert Farms, Oliver

Derek is the Hospitality & Sales Manager at Covert Farms. He works with local chefs advising them on creating menus with Covert's local farm ingredients as well as being an ambassador for the farm. He is also the Farm Chef, on site to cater dinners.

Originally from Victoria, Derek has 21 years of experience in the food and beverage industry. In 2006 Derek and his wife Sunnie opened Piggys BarBQ in Penticton BC for three successful summers. For the last four years Derek worked in Albania as a Chef and Medic in an exploration camp allowing for the exploration of Spanish and Italian wine regions and undiscovered Eastern European varietals.

In his own words:
"Cooking in the valley is different for two reasons. First because it is not manufactured. We don't just say we love the country or enjoy the outdoors. We live here and are the lifestyle.

Second is the bounty of the Okanagan is overwhelming. I am often asked what I did to make the salad taste so great. The answer is, 'It was picked this morning.' The ingredients speak for themselves.

Okanagan cuisine is dining "in place". That is an idea we really enjoy exploring at Covert Farms. Out motto is "cultivating enjoyment". To eat the farm produce and fruits that are grown side by side with the wine you're drinking while you look at the view and feel the same sun and breeze that the food did. That is my idea of farm to fork."

THE FARMER

Gene Covert, Covert Farms, Oliver

In 1959 George Covert, part owner of Hayman & Covert Tomato Packing Company in Tracy, California first heard of the Okanagan while talking to his broker in Calgary, who mentioned a truck load of apricots from Oliver, BC. Intrigued by a climate suitable to grow soft fruit and vegetables in Canada, George came to the Okanagan Valley to see for himself. On a weekend trip in the dead of winter, he discovered and purchased the undeveloped mesa north of Oliver that was to become Covert Farms.

In 1961 George brought his wife Winnifred, and their two sons, Calvin and Michael, to Oliver to start their new Canadian life and Covert Farms.

Mike's son Gene and his wife Shelly Covert have transformed Covert Farms' over 600 acres into an amazing agri tourism and agri-entertainment destination. They remain a major shipper of fresh field tomatoes, sweet onions, sweet corn, muskmelons and table grapes. They also make organic, award-winning wine, featuring new labels with a new name - Covert Farms Family Estate Winery. The farm offers an on-site fruit and vegetable stand with a u-pick option, organic fruit and fun activities for the kids including a corn maze and farm mini golf. The Coverts have also set up a CSA (Community Supported Agriculture) which is a partnership between producer and consumer. Members sign up to purchase a share of the current season's harvest up front. Each week, members receive a box of the freshest local and seasonal organic produce available.

They also are sharing that knowledge with the next generation through their Young Organic Farmers camps.

In his own words:
"We are about great food and the relationships that are necessary to bring that about in a sustainable way. We are by no means the experts. Organic … Bio-dynamic … Permaculture … The relationships of our land are many and complex and most have yet to be discovered. As we do though, we find interest, intrigue, humility and of course great food. We see farming as a responsibility to balance the use of our land with the needs of our society. This is not an easy task. Farming in the last 80 years has become industrialized to the point that we are just extracting the soil, leaving scars on the land and polluting our waterways. This is not sustainable.

Good food is not just about taste. It's about place. A healthy place. A place that is nurtured and respected will return great food. The cornerstone of sustainable farming is soil. Soil is a living, breathing organism. Given proper care and attention healthy soil can feed your crops, lessen water stress and reduce harmful plant diseases. Beyond soil there is the rest of the environment, on farm and surrounding, that needs to be maintained in balance. Careful observation and thoughtful experimentation can work to develop the biodiversity that is crucial to a healthy system."

PAIRING

2009 Amicitia - Covert Farms Family Estate Winery

(ah-mee-CHEE-tee-ah) is Latin for friends – making this a wonderful name for a blend. A camaraderie emerges from this amicable blend of Cabernet Sauvignon, Cabernet Franc, Syrah, Petit Verdot, Malbec, Merlot and Zinfandel. Complex and well-balanced with notes of Black Forest cake, vanilla and wild berries following through with plums and spiced dark fruits on the palate.

CITRUS SOCKEYE SALMON

CHEF: LIAM McNULTY, NK'MIP PATIO RESTAURANT, OSOYOOS
FISHERY: OKANAGAN NATION ALLIANCE, OSOYOOS
WINEMAKER: NK'MIP CELLARS, OSOYOOS

The story of the Sockeye salmon's return to the Okanagan Valley is dramatic. This recipe is a fresh and delicious celebration of this beautiful fish as well as the aboriginal history of the Osoyoos Indian Band and Nk'Mip Cellars. After years of conservation efforts to restore the salmon stocks in the Okanagan River, ONA Fisheries are opening its boats to the public to take part in Eco-fishing tours. Enjoy the local First Nation's knowledge of (N'tytyix) Sockeye Salmon and hear Chaptik stories of the lands, the legends, and the people.

1 fillet of local Sockeye Salmon, skin on, pin bones removed
3 tbsp sea salt
3 tbsp sugar
3 tbsp lemon zest
3 tbsp orange zest
1 tbsp toasted fennel seeds, ground
2 tbsp Chardonnay (local suggestion: Nk'Mip Chardonnay)

Place the salmon skin side down in a plastic container large enough to hold the whole salmon. Combine dry ingredients and sprinkle over top of the salmon and then pour the wine over. Cover with plastic wrap and let cure in the fridge 24 hours. The fish will be ready when it is firm to the touch. Remove and thinly slice.

Flax Seed Crackers:
2 cups whole flax seed
1 cup ground flax seed
1 tbsp olive oil
1 tbsp fresh rosemary, chopped
1 1/2 cups water

Blend all ingredients into a smooth paste. Spread on a parchment lined sheet pan in a thin layer. Bake at 300°F for about an hour or until firm. Cut or break into desired cracker size or if you prefer a uniform size, score the desired shape before baking.

"Boursin" Cheese Spread:
1/2 cup butter, room temperature
1/2 cup goat cheese
1/2 cup (mixture of) parsley, basil and chives, chopped
zest of 1/2 lemon
salt and pepper to taste

Blend with paddle attachment or electric mixer for 6-8 minutes until fluffy. Serve on flax crackers topped with a citrus sockeye slice.

THE CHEF

Liam McNulty, Nk'Mip Patio Restaurant, Osoyoos

Described by friends as a man with a "meticulous Don Draper haircut and wildly authoritative hand gestures that is like an infant with his toys when you put him around food." A self-trained cook from Alberta, Liam became attached to the Spirit Ridge Resort by first helping to found Passa Tempo Restaurant at Spirit Ridge, he later moved on to head up its partner restaurant in the Nk'Mip Cellars Winery.

Liam's food has been described as rustic and heart-warming with its family-style focus on rich, savoury comfort meals. He sources all of his ingredients locally.

In his own words:
"Why I love the Okanagan? Knowing that I can pick something from a tree, or dig into the earth for food and have it in my belly within minutes, hours, not days or weeks. I love getting the real nutritional value from a local tomato, rather then one that is genetically engineered and picked two weeks early, ripened with gas and then shipped across North America.

Farmers are key. I wouldn't have a job without hard working farmers and ranchers.

I have always been the type of person to get to know the area I live in so I check out farms and source local purveyors. Many of the suppliers I use I have met through other chefs, the farmers market scene and wrong turns down dusty gravel roads..."

THE FISHERY

Okanagan Nation Alliance, Osoyoos

Did you know that once upon a time we had salmon living in Okanagan Lake? I sat down with Jon Crofts from Codfathers Seafood Market in Kelowna for a history lesson on this incredible fish and the efforts being made to stabilize and rebuild the declining wild Okanagan Sockeye population and revitalize the Okanagan Nation Alliance salmon fishery.

In the mid-1800's, the Sockeye fishery began to change dramatically with the arrival of European traders and ranchers. Settlement along the river, the building of dams, channelization, commercial fishing, irrigation and domestic water use damaged salmon habitat, interrupted migration routes, reduced stocks entering the rivers to spawn, increased competition for the resource and destroyed traditional fishing sites.

The Okanagan River is the largest of three remaining Columbia River Sockeye runs. Of the total Sockeye that return to the Columbia Basin, over 80% are Okanagan stock. Since the 1990's, the Okanagan Sockeye escapement has fluctuated between 5,000 and 210,000. Years when only a few thousand Sockeye returned to the spawning grounds had conservationists fearing for its extinction.

Through the conservation work of the ONA (Okanagan Nations Alliance) and favourable environmental conditions – a record sockeye Salmon run of 500,000 returned this year! The goal is to continue this work allowing the salmon population back in to Skaha Lake and then hopefully Okanagan Lake. Can you imagine? One day we may be able to enjoy Sockeye salmon in Okanagan Lake.

Jon and Anne-Marie Crofts have become involved with this conservation work and have signed an agreement with the ONA allowing Jon to process and distribute the salmon in the valley. "This is a really good thing for the valley. It's not very often that you get to see such a dramatic effect following conservation efforts." Jon wants "to make sure that the fish are respected, taken care of and managed locally," and comments that this initiative will also "secure this local food source for the valley for years to come."

THE WINEMAKER

Nk'Mip Cellars, Osoyoos

Nk'Mip Cellars (pronounced in-ka-meep) is North America's first Aboriginal owned and operated winery lead by Chief Clarence Louie. Winemaker Randy Picton produces Pinot Blanc, Riesling, Chardonnay, Pinot Noir, Merlot, Cabernet Sauvignon, Syrah, Riesling Icewine and a blended Meritage. These grapes come from the Band's own Inkameep Vineyard as well as the vineyard located adjacent to the winery. "We have the utmost respect for our surrounding lands that we rely so heavily on to give us our quality grapes. It is wonderful that we can give back through the resulting wines," says Picton.

Randy Picton

PAIRING

Nk'Mip Quam Qwmt Chardonnay

Medium-bodied, aromas of buttered toast mingle with Okanagan tree fruits like apple and pear. Finishes with a pleasant zip of citrus.

Fig & Blue Cheese Ravioli

Chef: Jeremy Luypen, Owner/Chef Terrafina Restaurant, Oliver
Cheesemaker: Gitta Pedersen, Poplar Grove Cheese, Naramata
Winemaker: Hester Creek Winery, Oliver

Pasta, pasta, pasta! Everyone loves this gorgeous comfort food that is embraced in every season. Making it from scratch has to been one of life's more satisfying accomplishments and once you start, there is a threat that you will become an addict. So versatile, ravioli fillings are endless.

Ravioli Dough:
3 1/2 cups of Caputo Tipo '00' flour
5 eggs
2 tbsp tomato paste

Whisk eggs and tomato paste together. Put the flour on a clean countertop, make a large hole or well in the center of it, pour in egg mixture, with a fork slowly stir in the flour to the eggs, folding in the wall slowly until the dough gets stiff enough to use your hands. Knead dough till a smooth ball, note that it might not take all the flour. Wrap up dough in plastic wrap and rest for 30 min.

Filling:
6 fresh figs
4 oz goat cheese
5 oz blue cheese
1 bunch organic spinach
1 tsp chopped garlic
1 tsp chopped shallots
3 tbsp Okanagan dry white wine

Finely dice figs, crumble both cheeses. In a sauté pan cook garlic and shallots, add in spinach cook for 3 minutes on medium. Deglaze with white wine.
Place cheese and figs in large bowl, add in the sautéed spinach and mix with the cheese.

Using a pasta roller to gauge size, roll out pasta dough starting on number 1, then moving to number 3 and finish on number 5, egg wash one side of the pasta dough, place about a teaspoon of filling on the dough, place a sheet over top and cut into circles, press the edges together. Cook in boiling salted water for 3 to 5 minutes. For sauce it is up to you, Jeremy likes a simple rendered down pancetta or North Okanagan Game Meats bacon with butter. Mmmmm.

Local Suggestions:
Blue Cheese -Poplar Grove Cheese, Naramata
Happy Days Goat Cheese, Salmon Arm
Eggs - Urban Harvest, Kelowna
Spinach - Harker's Organics, Similkameen
Pork Belly for bacon - North Okanagan Game Meats, Enderby
Figs, Flour, Tomato Paste- Valoroso Foods, Kelowna
Wine - Hester Creek Winery Pinot Gris

Jeremy Luypen and
Gitta Pedersen

THE CHEF

Jeremy Luypen, Executive Chef/Co-owner, Terrafina Restaurant, Oliver

Jeremy Luypen was born in the Fraser Valley of BC. At a young age he already knew that he enjoyed cooking for friends and family. A graduate from the Culinary Arts Program at Okanagan University College in Kelowna, Jeremy honed his skills at several restaurants in BC and Calgary before the opportunity to co-own Terrafina came up in 2011. A dream come true, he and business partner April Goldade opened their restaurant Terrafina in May of the same year. Terrafina means 'from the earth' in Italian – an appropriate name to match their philosophy of supporting local farmers and artisans.

In his own words
"The Okanagan is a dream for a chef and it is getting better every year. I use as many locally sourced ingredients as possible and am always searching for new connections. Some suppliers bring us their products to try, others we source through needs of the menu. In the end, we use the best we can find. Sometimes that means a small fruit and produce stand at the side of the road with the nicest old couple that have owned it for 30 years. You can't help but walk away and smile knowing that the money you spent went to the right person for the right cause.

I describe Okanagan cuisine as simple, clean with fresh flavours. We are in wine country so it is our job to compliment the wine, have the wine complement the food and offer that healthy balance. For the future of our food and wine world I hope for a more sustainable industry - going back to the old days of farming. "

THE CHEESEMAKER

Gitta Pedersen, Poplar Grove Cheese, Naramata

Originally from Denmark, Gitta had a love of pediatric nursing that evolved into farming and eventually cheesemaking. She is a pioneer in our Okanagan cheese making world.

In her own words

"I grew up in Denmark on a farm, learning to appreciate growing and making your own food from the basics. Growing up I did not plan to get into farming myself; instead, I went through school wanting very much to become a nurse. After finishing my nursing degree in Denmark, I went travelling for a few months, and ended up here in Canada in 1990.

My spare time was spent on the farm we purchased, cutting down apple trees and replacing them with vines. I enjoyed the early years of the growing wine industry here in the Okanagan, starting Poplar Grove Winery from our small grape production. As the wine industry and tourism in the valley grew, the desire to start a cheesery was born. Coming from Denmark where cheese production (and consumption) is fairly high, I have always been interested in learning the process of cheese making. I have always loved all kinds of cheeses, the more flavourful and creamy cheeses being my favourites. So with a few recipes on hand, we started practicing our skills in the kitchen and soon moved into an addition to the winery. The early days were filled with lots of 'trials and errors,' but we soon got a following and the rest is history. My cheese facility remains very small, and the production is completely hands on, in which we feel we better control the outcome. We have continued to make the same four cheeses we started out with, my philosophy being that I would much rather make a few products really well than produce 15 different 'mediocre' cheeses. Also, in keeping it small, we continue to enjoy the benefits of a 'family' operation, where my cheese girls are essential in the quality of our production.

I continue to grow grapes on my farm, selling them to nearby high quality wineries.

In the last three years my pride and joy has been the addition of my son, Erich. He has spent his early years driving the tractor and watching milk being made into cheeses. He is already appreciating eating all kind of cheeses, hopefully he will continue to enjoy the same upbringing as I did myself."

THE WINEMAKER

Hester Creek Estate Winery, Oliver

This 22,000 square foot winery holds a bit of magic itself, as it is actually built into the mountainside. A unique and totally eco-friendly building design, the bunker style is to leave a "smaller footprint" on the native topography. Veteran Winemaker Summers, the former national Winemaker for Andrés Wines, runs the 35,000-case winery with ease. "The terroir on the Golden Mile allows grapes to express true varietal character, with intensity and crisp, vibrant flavours. It really allows the characteristics of the grapes to shine through." The winery property owned by Curt Garland also offers six deluxe villas as well as being home to Terrafina, a Tuscan-style restaurant, laden with some of the valley's oldest vines (44 years). The winery now offers food and wine experiences that includes tours, tastings and cooking classes.

Winemaker
Rob Summers (L) and
GM Mark Sheridan

PAIRING

2008 Hester Creek Estate Winery Reserve Merlot

A perfect match for Terrafina – this rich Merlot is earthy. Chocolate layers with spice notes and dark fruit loll on the palate and express the depth that comes from the 35-year-old vines from which it was made.

HALIBUT DOLMATHES

CHEF: TARA BUCHMAN, THE KITCHENETTE, SILK SCARF WINERY, SUMMERLAND
FARMER: SILK SCARF VINEYARDS, SUMMERLAND
WINEMAKER: SILK SCARF WINERY, SUMMERLAND

If you have had the pleasure to dine on Tara's innovative, out-of-this-world cuisine you will understand its uniqueness. It is a combination of flavours from her culinary roots in Israel fused with the taste of the Okanagan – she says "it is a hybrid of all things that I am." Tara chooses the grape leaves carefully, picking the newer growth for tenderness – these leaves are thinner. The leaves are incredibly versatile and can be preserved. Tara suggests using them in different ways as a wrapping for cheese or fish before grilling. She also suggests wrapping fresh goat cheese in grape leaves, drizzling with honey and then grilling– mmmm.

Ingredients:
10 grape leaves
(local suggestion: Find a friend with a vineyard)

Filling:
250g finely chopped skinless wild halibut fillet
1/3 cup chopped Italian parsley
1/3 cup chopped cilantro
1/3 cup chopped red onion
1-2 crushed garlic cloves
zest from 1/2 lemon
3 tsp freshly squeezed lemon juice
1 egg white
2 tbsp rice flour
2 tsp sumac
1/4 tsp salt
2 pinches of white pepper

For serving :
kefir or yogurt
1 ripe tomato cut in half
pickled turnips (see recipe on our website www. anokanagancookbook.com)

Preparing the Grape Leaves:
Pick tender and shiny new growth leaves that are big enough for filling. Using scissors, cut off stems. Blanch in boiling salted water for 1 minute, or until the leaves change their color. Drain and set aside to and cool off.

Halibut filling:
Combine all the ingredients and chill for 30 minutes.

Preparing the Dolmathes:
Carefully lay out one grape leaf on a flat surface with the veins facing upward and the stem end towards you. Place 1 heaping tbsp of the halibut mixture near the stem end of the leaf.
Start by folding the bottom of the leaf over the filling, then fold both sides toward the middle, and finish by rolling into a tight bundle. Repeat with the rest of the leaves. Preheat a grill or a grill pan for medium heat, oil well and grill the dolmathes for 7-10 minutes, flipping halfway through.
For serving, spread the kefir/yogurt on a plate, place the hot dolmathes on top and squeeze the tomato over the dish.

Note: If using preserved grape leaves, blanching is not necessary. Simply soak in plenty of cold water for 30 minutes, then drain.

THE CHEF

Tara Buchman, The Kitchenette, Silk Scarf Winery, Summerland

Tara came to the Okanagan one summer on vacation with a vague plan of drinking good wine and picking cherries at the Manoffs' farm (family friends from Israel.) Never did she imagine that she would fall madly in love with Summerland and its bounty and leave her home to move here.

Tara is a passionate chef whose creativity and international tasting experience results in outstanding original dishes.

In her own words:
Tara explains, "food is not only about fashion" or what is trending. She explains her creative process: "Every year you meet your seasonal ingredients again after missing them for a while and try to invent new ways to use them." Tara believes there is "a lot of storytelling in cooking. After I serve my food, I come out to meet the people and I am at a loss for what to say because I feel that I have already said everything through my food." This romantic vision of chefs and the passion they put into preparing their food is very moving and testament to the artistry and passion that goes into the culinary arts.

Tara would like to see more chefs "making food that tells their unique story – it would include tastes from their personal history, and new creations that doesn't necessarily try to conform to one specific style." This way "the eating experience will broaden the diner's thinking and become more inspiring for all."

The creation of The Kitchenette was a delicious gift of love to our wine country. Tara and the Manoffs wanted to share their vision of the Okanagan with us. "This is how food and wine should be enjoyed: under the sun, with friends in a casual atmosphere."

THE WINEMAKER /FARMER

Silk Scarf Winery, Summerland

Roie Manoff spent 26 years in the Israeli Air Force as an Israeli fighter jet pilot. His retirement from this intense line of work brought him to the sunny Okanagan where he and his wife Ruth purchased an apple orchard that would become Silkscarf's vineyard in 2004. Since then Roie and his son/co-Winemaker Idan have crafted award-winning wines.

In his own words:
"The Okanagan wine industry is a relatively young industry, thus it is still quite vibrant and keeps striving for improvement. That generates a lot of creativity and innovation in both wine making as well as in the wine hospitality arena.

The wineries are very 'open' to one another ready to share ideas and information among themselves, in a positive collegial way, therefore generating a constant improvement in wine quality.

The differences between Israel's wine industry and the Okanagan's are mainly due to the difference in climates. Israel is a warm climate wine region where the Okanagan is a cool climate region. Wine has been produced in Israel since biblical times. The Okanagan wine industry is a young-new world industry.

In warm climate regions the growing season is longer – basically, there are no marginal seasons. Any grape type can be grown there with no serious considerations.

A primary concern in Israeli wine production is maintaining acid levels to balance the naturally high sugars that the warm climate of the region produces. In Canada it is the other way around - acid levels are usually on the high mark and sugar levels are relatively difficult to gain."

PAIRING

2011 Silk Scarf Viognier

Heavenly aromas of Okanagan stone fruit on the nose. Peaches and nectarines follow through to the palate with a rich mouthfeel and hints of spice. A beautiful wine that pairs well with food or to sip alone. "It is an excellent summer wine."

Heirloom Tomato Salad

CHEF: Natasha Schooten, Terrafina Restaurant, Oliver
FARMER: Harker's Organics, Cawston
WINEMAKER: Rustic Roots Winery, Cawston

The return of the heirloom tomato varieties could arguably be one of the most important renaissances in the history of taste. The variety of shapes, sizes and flavours of this vegetable (botanically it is actually a fruit) and versatility in its use make it a key ingredient in many cultures. Many quiver with anticipation each year for their colourful return to the markets and make a point of eating them every day, in every way and preserving them into sauce for the winter. For this recipe, Chef Natasha has beautifully presented her favorite local ingredient, Harker's heirloom tomatoes, as well as cleverly pairing it with fruit wine from Harker's winery – Rustic Roots. Summerland Vinegar Works is also in the spotlight – no need to leave the valley to get balsamico vinegar –we've got it all here.

Yield: 4 Salads

Salad:
4 large heirloom tomatoes, cut into quarters
1 ball (175 g) buffalo mozzarella, torn into 12 pieces

Balsamico Reduction:
Yield: 1/4 cup

Ingredients:
3/4 cup red wine vinegar (local suggestion: Balsamico Rosso, Vinegar Works, Summerland)
1 1/2 cups of white balsamic vinegar (local suggestion: Balsamico Bianca, Vinegar Works, Summerland)
4 cups Port (local suggestion: Dirty Laundry Vineyards "A Girl In Every" Port)
2 tbsp local honey

Method:
Put both the vinegars in a large saucepan and bring to rapid simmer until the liquid is reduced by 1/3. Add the Port and keep reducing at rapid simmer rate. When liquid is reduced by 1/2, add in the honey and reduce until a syrupy consistency is achieved. Store at room temperature until ready to use.

To serve:
Using a pastry brush "paint" a line of reduction across the bottom of each plate. Add two pieces of tomato and three pieces of buffalo mozzarella, arranging, as you like.
Top with a nice kosher salt and a little canola oil, then finish with the balsamico reduction.

THE CHEF

Natasha Schooten, Terrafina Restaurant, Oliver

Originally from the small town of Nanton, Alberta, Natasha began her career studying Culinary Arts at the SAIT Polytechnic in Calgary. After spending seven years with Delta Hotels and Resorts in locations across Canada, she landed at the Mission Hill Family Estate Winery in Kelowna. From there, Natasha advanced to Chef de Cuisine at Osoyoos' Watermark Resort where she spent the last couple of years before joining Terrafina Restaurant.

In her own words:

"When I was working at Mission Hill Winery in 2008 the philosophy on food and the terroir that (former Winery Chef) Michael Allemeier was instilling in his chefs was a major awakening for me and this is what keeps me here as well as getting to work with wonderful producers like the Harker family and of course the wineries. I love the interaction that we as chefs get with our producers and farmers and the fresh products that you 'can't wait for' like heirloom tomatoes and that ability we have as chefs to showcase these amazing products to our customers and tell the stories. I think the biggest changes that we can do as chefs and consumers is to: eat with the seasons, demand that our grocery stores buy local and support local farmers and producers, and educate ourselves on where our food is coming from. I think Okanagan cuisine is best described by using fresh local ingredients that are in season in a simplistic manner to let the food and the freshness shine through."

THE FARMER/ WINEMAKER

Sara Harker - Harker's Organics/Rustic Roots Winery, Cawston

"Our philosophy on farming is: To sustain our multi generational organic family farm and business through diversity of crops and value added entities that secure local organic food and entice many generations to continue the Harker legacy!"
- Sara Harker

The Harker (née Manery) family settled in the Similkameen Valley and began farming in 1888. Five generations of this family business have thrived and with the current one raising the sixth generation and now making organic fruit wine, they are taking the legacy to a new level. The ancient snow apple or Fameuse tree planted in the early 1900's still stands today on the Harker Organic Farm and is a proud symbol for the Harker family of their pioneer heritage.

James Manery, along with his wife, traveled west on horseback from Ontario in 1868. They settled in the Similkameen Valley where William managed the Old Barcelo Ranch. Their first of ten children, Samuel James Manery, was born on March 14th, 1888. He was the fourth non-native baby born in the Similkameen.

Kathy and Bruce Harker are passionate about practicing sustainable organic agriculture. They are proud of the evolution of their multi-generational family farm and that all of their children are involved in the family business.

Winemaker Sara Harker's venture into winemaking was initiated through her passion for supporting the local economy and maintaining her belief in sustainability. Instead of going the grape wine route she thought, "Why not make wine with what we already have?" With the Harker's thriving orchards at her fingertips, Sara went to work on capturing the essence of the tree fruits in a bottle. A true taste of summer in every drop, these creative flavour bombs will send your taste buds to a whole new level.

PAIRING

2010 Rustic Roots Apple Pear Fruit Wine

Made with a blend of five varieties of Certified Organic apples and three varieties of Certified Organic pears. This fresh, crisp wine has the aroma of crisp apples with a finish of pear, spice and herbs.

MORTADELLA & PICKLED GARLIC SCAPE TORTELLINI IN HAM HOCK BRODO

CHEF: COURTENAY WELTER, MIRADORO RESTAURANT AT TINHORN CREEK, OLIVER
FARMER: MELANIE NOVAK, MICHELLE AND MILAN STARCIC, GROWN WITH LOVE GARLIC FARM, OLIVER
WINEMAKER: TINHORN CREEK VINEYARDS, OLIVER

This rich and flavourful dish will soothe your soul. Featuring the arrival of the beautiful garlic scapes in the springtime, Courtenay suggests pickling and canning the rest to use later in the year. Check our website, www.anokanagancookbook.com, for a garlic scape pickling recipe from Michelle at Grown With Love Garlic Farm. Mortadella is an Italian cured sausage, resembling bologna in size and appearance. It is made of pork that is first ground and then mashed into a paste, and may get its name from the Roman word for 'mortar.'

Ingredients:
2 smoked ham hocks (local suggestion: Illichmann's Delicatessan, Kelowna)
1 carrot peeled
2 stalks celery
2 yellow onions
1 bay leaf
5 black peppercorns
sherry vinegar to taste
salt to taste

Place ham hocks in heavy bottomed pot and add enough water to cover hocks by 2 inches. Bring to simmer, and skim off the scum that floats to the surface.
Roughly chop vegetables, add to pot with peppercorns and bay leaf. Bring to simmer.
Simmer for 3 hours, skimming when necessary.
Filter broth through fine mesh strainer. Season with salt and sherry vinegar to taste.
Cool and refrigerate until the fat comes to the surface and solidifies. Discard the fat.
Reserve some of the meat for tortellini filling.

Pasta Dough:
300g all purpose flour
3 eggs

Place above ingredients in a food processor, blend until consistency of sand. Turn out onto floured surface, bring dough together, and knead until smooth. Let rest half an hour. Once filling is made, roll out dough according to directions on pasta machine, finishing on thinnest setting.

Mortadella & Garlic Scape Filling:
125g mortadella, finely chopped
125g ham hock finely chopped (reserved from making broth),
100g swiss chard, finely chopped, blanched and drained
150g ricotta cheese
50g Parmesan cheese, grated
75g sweet pickled garlic scapes, finely chopped
1 egg
75g fine breadcrumbs
(add more if filling seems too wet)
salt and black pepper to taste

Mix above ingredients together, and season with salt and black pepper to taste.
Filling should be thick, and hold together.

Assembly:
Using a 2" round cookie cutter, cut rounds out of rolled pasta sheets. Place 1/4 to 1/2 tsp filling in centre of rounds. Fold each circle in half, and press the edges firmly together with your fingertips. Pick up tortellini, with folded edge facing down, wrap tortellini around index finger until the two edges meet. Press firmly together. Flip the outer edge of the tortellini away from you to create a ridge. Place on flour lined baking sheet.
Bring pot of salted water to boil. Cook tortellini for 1-2 minutes, or until pasta is al dente.
Place 5-7 tortellini in warm bowl, and cover with hot, seasoned ham hock broth. Garnish with more pickled garlic scapes. Serve.

(L-R) Chef Courtenay Welter, Michelle Starcic, Melanie Novak and Milan Starcic

THE CHEF

Courtenay Welter, Sous Chef, Miradoro Restaurant at Tinhorn Creek, Oliver

Courtenay trained under Vancouver's super Chef Rob Clark of C-Restaurant before joining Chef Jeff Van Geest at his Vancouver Aurora Restaurant. Reunited now with Van Geest, both are blazing the Okanagan terroir with their distinctly Okanagan cuisine. Both are dedicated to eating local, drinking local and supporting local farmers and producers nearby their restaurant in Oliver.

Courtenay loves her new life in the Okanagan and feels she is "living a Chef's dream being submerged deep into wine country and surrounded by farmers."

In her own words:
"I moved to the Okanagan originally to assist Chef Jeff Van Geest with the opening of Miradoro Restaurant at Tinhorn Creek. I wasn't intending to stay; I just wanted to take a break from the city, to be anonymous, and to try to heal a recently broken heart. That was over a year ago; I have since chosen to settle in the Okanagan. It is

paradise for a cook. I can literally look across the valley from the restaurant kitchen, and see where our food comes from. I know many of our farmers by name.

I see the South Okanagan culinary scene continuing to grow. I see our local farms continuing to establish themselves, to become known as the hub for quality organic food. I hope that restaurants in this area continue to help and support each other, sharing suppliers, sharing cooks, even sharing delivery drivers - working together. The seasonality of our business thrives on that. There is no competition in this valley, just a large group of like-minded, good-hearted people, doing what they love.

I would like to thank Adam Pegg of La Quercia restaurant in Vancouver. He spent 1.5 years training me on the art of pasta making. I give all my credit to him. He is an incredible teacher, a tough critic, and the one man I would be as honored, as I would be terrified, to cook for."

THE FARMER

Grown with Love Garlic Farm, Melanie Novak, Michelle and Milan Starcic, Oliver

Grown With Love Garlic Farm is a small, family run farm in Oliver. Farmed by Milan and Michelle Starcic and Melanie Novak, it started with little more than a garden, selling from a small farm stand by the roadside. Over the last couple years they have selected the tastiest and most vigorous types of garlic for their farm. Coupled with keeping the finest seed and meticulous organic practices, not to mention a lot of love, they are happy to offer four of the finest organic garlic varieties: Alban, Red Russian, Inchelium Red and Music.

In Michelle's words:
"We chose garlic as a possibly pest resistant crop amidst many other crops in the Okanagan Valley. We love growing garlic because it seems to be a food that most people LOVE. It has many beneficial health properties and can be used in many wonderful ways. We enjoy working directly with chefs because we then know that all our hard work will be utilized in the most fantastic culinary ways possible. We love to sell as close to home as possible. I have been selling produce at farmers' markets for three years now. I feel a huge demand more and more for fresh organic, local produce. The love of wonderful fresh food is coming back into our lives and culture. I see the demand for more fresh items each year, such as eggs, meats, cheeses, and mostly fruit and vegetables."

THE WINEMAKER

Tinhorn Creek Vineyards, Oliver

Sandra Oldfield

Tinhorn Creek Vineyards is legendary for its sustainability practice and super green operating methods. Owners Ken and Sandra Oldfield (also Winemaker) continually strive to improve their efficient, earth-friendly winegrowing operation. Known as the "Compost Queen", Sandra Oldfield has become a role model for other Okanagan vineyards to adopt their policy to reduce its carbon footprint.

Their revolution started back in 2004 when Tinhorn began releasing beetles to control a particular weed (the beetles eat the stems) to replace the use of herbicides. Over the years they have installed snake fences to protect the endangered snakes from people, converted fuel usage to biodiesel to operate farm machinery, installed a super efficient drip irrigation system that not only cuts down water usage, but has also had a positive effect on the vines that naturally don't like to be wet because it promotes disease – this way, they have cut down on spraying. Basically the Oldfields are green machines – and, they make great wine to boot.

PAIRING

2011 Oldfield Series 2Bench Rosé

This is a perfect brunch Rosé. Made in the Mediterranean style, this dry, crisp Rosé with a red berry nose is made from 100% Cabernet Franc. Because of its popularity, Sandra upped production to 1300 cases in 2012.

Purselane Salad w/ Local Cherries, Radishes & Bell Peppers With Cucumber, Lime Vinaigrette & Toasted Pecans

Chef: Justin Paakkunainen, Walnut Beach Resort, Osoyoos
Farmer: Fernandes Farms, Osoyoos
Winemaker: Wild Goose Vineyards, Okanagan Falls

Purselane is an interesting, delicious substitute for lettuce in a salad. It is actually from the succulent family and is a common invasive weed in North America, particularly in Californian vineyards. The stems, leaves and flower buds are edible and are delicious raw in a salad or cooked in stir-fries or used in lieu of spinach. Packed with vitamins, minerals and antioxidants, purselane is higher in Omega 3 fatty acids than any other land plant!

Serves 4

1 bunch of purselane, cut to bite size pieces
1/2 red bell pepper, cut into thin strips
1/2 yellow bell pepper, cut into thin strips
1/2 red onion, sliced thin
15-20 cherries, pitted
5 radishes, sliced thin
1 cup pecans, toasted

Dressing:
1/2 cup cucumber, seeded and finely grated
3 limes, zest from 1 and juice from all 3
3 tbsp gin (local suggestion: Okanagan Spirits Gin)
2 tbsp honey
1/4 cup olive oil
a pinch of salt and pepper

Whisk all ingredients together in a bowl and set aside.
Place all ingredients except for the pecans in a large salad bowl. Toss with the cucumber lime vinaigrette, top with pecans and enjoy!

L-R Chef Paakkunainen, Laura, Cidalia and Lucy Fernandes

THE CHEF

Justin Paakkunainen, Executive Chef, Walnut Beach Resort, Osoyoos

Originally from Thunder Bay, Ontario, Justin attended Toronto's George Brown College. His career path led him to restaurants in Alberta - including the Executive Chef position at Elkwater Lake Lodge. Now happily at the helm of the Walnut Beach Resort kitchen, Paakkunainen notes that Walnut Beach has recently become the first licensed beach in Canada allowing guests to order right out to tables next to their lakeside lounging chairs. "My focus is on a menu that is local, healthy and fresh". He sources as many local products as he can for his creations, and loves to suggest pairings with a variety of South Okanagan wines.

In his own words:
"The opportunity to work with fresh local ingredients at home and in the restaurant, as well as being able to broaden my horizons on the infinite varieties of wines available drew me to the Okanagan.

My favorite local ingredient would have to be the peach. Not only is it delicious on its own, it is fantastic in a large variety of ways. Grilled and served with ice cream and granola, peach salsa on grilled chicken or salmon, or even a peach and honey vinaigrette on a fresh summer salad. What I see happening with our culinary scene is the growing population of locavores. With all of the fantastic local products we have at our fingertips it would be a shame if we didn't. I could also see more wineries opening restaurants, and creating good opportunities for young chefs like myself and other chefs in the area."

THE FARMER

The Fernandes Family, Fernandes Farms, Osoyoos

Joe and Maria Fernandes arrived in Osoyoos from Madeira, Portugal in 1959. Over the last 40 years the Fernandes family has built a large farming business that includes orchards, a fruit stand and a big family. "Joe remembers growing bananas, sugar cane, and other tropical fruit in Portugal and he dreamed of doing the same thing here." And he did.
In 1980 Joe built the only banana farm in all of Canada!

In a large hot house Joe planted over 500 banana trees, sugar cane, lemon and orange trees and many other exotic plants. When Joe passed away, sadly the exotic fruit business closed but now his seven children (Helen, Laura, Lucy, Joe, Cidalia, Tom and Greg Fernandes) run the Fruit stand business, featuring local fruit and vegetables. Their farm still includes a vegetable hot house where local fruit and vegetables are sold to the wholesale market.

THE WINEMAKER

Wild Goose Vineyards, Okanagan Falls

This award-winning family-run winery has become synonymous with outstanding examples of the German varietals like Riesling and Gewürztraminer. In 1983 founder Adolf Kruger purchased a barren piece of land east of Okanagan Falls where he discovered a large flock of Canada geese feeding in amongst the tumbleweeds, boulders, and rubble. As he approached, the flock of geese took flight and flew to the north. From this time on, the property became known as Wild Goose Vineyards.
Wild Goose was established in June 1990 when the first production of Riesling, Gewürztraminer, and Marechal Foch hit the marketplace. Adolf Kruger has passed the reins to his two sons, Winemaker Hagen Kruger and General Manager Roland Kruger, but is still involved in the winery.

Roland Kruger, in his own words:
"How times have changed over the years! The growth of the wine industry has been truly amazing over the last 20 years. Pushing over 225 wineries is an astonishing number for British Columbia. The quality of wine has also skyrocketed; every winery is producing high quality wines. It is truly exciting to see.

Along with the growth of our industry has been the growth and maturation of the local food industry. We are still a six-month destination, which makes it very challenging for some eateries here in the Okanagan. Obviously if you are a food provider in a larger city in the Okanagan, there is always the local market to help you through the sometimes challenging times off season. From the winery perspective it is amazing to see the quality of local foods being made here in the Okanagan. When customers are touring wineries, it is natural that a food element be attached to their touring. Wineries have tied into this by offering food services at Hester Creek, Tinhorn, Burrowing Owl, Quails Gate, to name only a few. Not only are they offering food… but the food quality is amazing with them using many locally grow ingredients. How exciting!
Away from the wine touring, restaurants have sprung up that produce wine country dining that raises cuisine to a new level. The cuisine in the Okanagan has really stepped up many notches over the years - just as the wines get better and better, so does the food!"

PAIRING

2011 Wild Goose Mystic River Pinot Gris

Grown on their Mystic River Vineyards in Oliver, these particular Pinot Gris vines were planted in 2006. This wine provides a mouthful of apricots and pears balanced with a crisp hit of acidity making it perfect for food pairings.

Quinoa Crusted Falafel Mignon

Chef: Jesse Croy, Sunset Bistro, Summerhill Pyramid Winery, Kelowna
Farmer: Gabe Cipes, Summerhill Organic Gardens, Kelowna
Winemaker: Summerhill Pyramid Winery, Kelowna

This starter recipe combines all of the organic magic that flows from the Summerhill grounds. The produce and the grapes grown on this Certified Organic land have created an oasis of health by the Cipes family. True to their brand, Chef Jesse has created a unique dish that is also vegetarian and celiac friendly thanks to the use of the beautiful quinoa grain. Jesse says, "I love play on words concepts and illustrating that you don't need to rely on fatty meats for flavour. I love meat as long as it's healthy, happy animals!"

Serves 6
(Vegetarian & Celiac Friendly)

Ingredients:
2 cups garbanzo beans (chick peas)
2 cups fresh English peas, shelled
1/4 cup chick pea flour
3 tbsp cilantro, fresh chopped
3 tbsp parsley, fresh chopped
3 tbsp mint, fresh chopped
2 green onions, chopped
1/4 cup red organic quinoa
1/2 cup water
3 cloves garlic, peeled
2 tbsp whole coriander seed
2 tbsp whole cumin seed
2 lemons
3 tbsp organic extra virgin olive oil
1 tbsp salt
1 tsp pepper
1 bunch rainbow chard

Tomato Tahini Emulsion:
2 heirloom tomatoes
2 tbsp tahini
1 clove garlic, peeled
2 lemons, juiced
1 tsp Dijon mustard
1 pinch salt
1/2 cup coconut oil

Place all ingredients into a blender and purèe while drizzling the coconut oil in slowly to emulsify. Set aside.

Cover the quinoa with the water and bring to a boil, remove from heat, cover and place on low burner for 20 minutes. Place the quinoa in a bowl to cool then fluff with fork.

Bring a pot of water to boil while cooking the quinoa, blanch the chard in the water for 30 seconds, leaving the leaves whole. Remove and place in ice water to cool. After chilled, dry the leaves and remove the large rib stem of the chard by cutting in half; this will become the wrap for the falafel. Use the same water to blanch the fresh peas (if they are still in season).

In a skillet, toast the cumin and coriander, crush in a mortar with pestle or spice grinder (Tip: coffee grinders work great).

Combine the garlic, oil, lemon juice and herbs and onion into a food processor and add the spices – blitz. Add in the peas, chick peas and chick pea flour and half the quinoa, pulse until combined. Form into filet mignon shaped "steaks," wrap each one with a ribbon of rainbow chard and press both sides into the red quinoa to form a crust. Chill for 1 hour.

To cook: sauté the vegan steaks in coconut oil or olive oil on medium-high heat in a cast iron skillet. Sear one side and flip, placing in a 350°F oven for 10 minutes. Serve with seasonal organic veggies and tomato tahini emulsion.

Chef Jesse Croy (R) and Eric von Krosigk

THE CHEF

Jesse Croy, Sunset Bistro, Summerhill Pyramid Winery, Kelowna

A childhood on a country lakeside farm instilled Croy's love for food and the power of food to be able to bring people together. In 2005, Jesse returned to Summerhill Winery as Sous Chef under Chef Grant de Montreuil, who assisted him in earning his Red Seal and becoming a CCFCC member. After two years of mentorship and introduction to local growers and artisans, the natural feel of honest, pure ingredients, familiar to country life, fuelled his passion further. Croy assumed the position of Executive Chef after de Montreuil's departure. Chef Croy is a firm believer in balancing simplicity and complexity when approaching the plate, ensuring the ingredient and its origin are always well respected.

In his own words:
"Not only is our local food delicious but by using local ingredients from our artisans and farmers we help stimulate our economy while raising awareness of the important role our food plays in bodily and community well being. We use organic suppliers who care deeply about how their product is grown. We must convey that level of respect through every step of the process until it arrives on the plate of our guests. Establishing a strong relationship with the farmers is paramount. Their contribution is instrumental and the beginning step in achieving excellence. Being flexible is a quality we both must share.

I fell in love with this paradise the first time I licked dripping warm peach juice off my elbow and got beach sand in my mouth while doing so. My cuisine is rooted in health as well as purity and honest flavours.

Okanagan cuisine is as pure as its amazing ingredients, those who respect them and those who provide them, helping to mold our cuisine into what it is today and what it will become.

I believe there is a definite change in the way people are enjoying food and drink today - its more down to earth and people care where their food comes from. Something old is always something new, just with a new coat of paint."

The Farmer

Gabe Cipes, Summerhill Organic Gardens, Kelowna

Gabe Cipes is a wild forager and organic farmer as well as being a musician.

In his own words:
"What inspires me to grow organically is that just about any solution to any problem can be found in nature. I love being a natural farmer. It is an endlessly fascinating world we live in.
Living and learning in the Okanagan is a great blessing. The more I learn of its history and great diversity of species, the more I realize how important this bio region is as a producer of food and medicine to the world and how it could naturally evolve back towards self sufficiency and food security.
I feel the future of our culinary scene or the future of organic farming will be to regenerate the wetlands/ watersheds/ natural diverse food producing ecosystems and re-establish some of the governance systems that allowed civilizations to thrive here pre-industrial revolution. I see Permaculture and Biodynamic practices

meshing with the Syilx ethical agriculture perspective and re-designing the conventional mono culture systems into technologically advanced poly culture systems that will be naturally resilient, sustainable and require zero chemical inputs."

The Winemaker

Summerhill Pyramid Winery, Kelowna

Famous for its pyramid built on the estate, Summerhill Pyramid Winery has become a leader in the Certified Organic grape growing movement. They say that their pyramid is second only to the Great Pyramid of Egypt for alignment and precision and was created without the use of any ferrous metals and remains aligned to the true north like the Great Pyramid itself.
Proving to the world that organic wine does indeed taste as good as non-organic, their leadership in creating their own micro-climate of Certified Organic land has set a standard for other growers to emulate.
Euro-trained Summerhill Winemaster Eric Von Krosigk is a minimalist winemaker and explains, "We're down to six things that we use to make wine with, and that includes the grapes and yeast."

Pairing

Summerhill Cipes Brut N/V

Perhaps the most recognized Okanagan bubbles, this Brut screams celebration! 100% Certified Organic, tiny bubbles tickle your nose and burst onto your palate with fresh Okanagan apples and a squeeze of pink grapefruit. Made in the traditional method, the Cipes Brut is Riesling and Chardonnay based. Crisp and fresh, these bubbles pair well with Okanagan life. It is a classic.

52

SUMMER SPICED PEPPER

CHEF: JAS DOSANJ, POPPADOMS – TASTE INDIA! RESTAURANT, KELOWNA
FARMER: WOLFGANG WESLE, GREEN CROFT GARDENS, GRINDROD
BREWMASTER: CANNERY BREWING, PENTICTON

Poppadoms Restaurant owners, the Dosanj family, moved here from the U.K. and have blessed us with their lighter, healthier version of Indian cuisine. The Dosanjs are also infusing our local flavours and products into their menu, creating a unique local version of Indian food. This light summer appetizer combines the sweetness of the Italian long red pepper with the subtle, savoury Indian flavours. This beautiful appetizer will make a dramatic start to any menu.

Serves 4

Prep Time: 15 minutes
Cooking Time: 20 minutes

Ingredients:
2 red Italian long sweet peppers (also called bull horn peppers. (local suggestion: Green Croft Gardens)
1 tbsp vegetable oil
1 tsp cumin seeds (local suggestion: Poppadom's spice kit)
1 small white onion (finely diced)
1 1/2 bell peppers (small dice, any colour) from Green Croft Gardens
110 g homemade paneer* (or buy from Indian shop) cut into 1 cm cubes
salt (to taste)
1/2 tsp. red chili powder
1 tsp garam masala (local suggestion: Poppadom's Spice Kit) or other masala blend

Homemade Paneer*:
1 litre 3.25% milk (local suggestion: Blackwell Dairy)
2 tbsp lemon juice, lime juice or vinegar
1 cheese cloth

Pour milk into a pot and boil on medium heat. Once boiled remove from heat and add the citrus to split the milk and stir. Empty into a cheesecloth. Place a weight on top of it to remove excess water. Prepare 2-3 hours before serving dish.

Method:
Wash the long peppers, dry, and slice in half. Remove seeds. Season the long peppers with a small pinch of salt, a sprinkle of cumin seeds and a drizzle of vegetable oil. Leave to one side. In a non-stick frying pan heat 1 tbsp vegetable oil on medium heat. Once oil is heated, add the cumin seeds and let crackle briefly.
Turn heat down to low, add onions along with 1/2 tsp salt (or to taste) and cook for approximately 5 minutes until soft but not brown.
Add diced bell peppers, followed by the red chili powder and garam masala. Stir together and cook for approximately 2 minutes. The bell peppers should be nice and crunchy. Mix in paneer and cook for another 2 minutes, stirring occasionally. Heat the grill or BBQ. Place the long pepper halves and grill both sides (approx. 2-3 minutes each side).
Once the long pepper is grilled, fill paneer mixture into pepper halves.
Enjoy.

THE CHEF

Jas Dosanj, Poppadoms- Taste India!, Kelowna

The Dosanj family moved to Kelowna from the UK in 2008 and opened up their restaurant: Poppadoms - Taste India! in 2009. This talented family has chef/mom Jas in the kitchen, daughter Aman handling marketing and PR, daughter Jasmin providing photography and creative, son Harry behind the bar and dad Serge overseeing the business. They have brought to Kelowna their innovative food (lower fat indian cuisine with a local gourmet spin) and their enthusiasm for bringing community together through fun events and theme parties.

In her own words:
"India is great for its regional local cooking, so whatever fresh produce is grown in a particular region is the staple, and that's what the Okanagan is about too. So, for us there is a natural fit between Indian food and using local Okanagan produce.
The idea behind Poppadoms is to create true-to-its-roots Indian food that's wholesome, fresh and healthy. We could only do that with great local raw ingredients, that's grown, raised or reared in a way we could feel good about it. Not only does our local produce taste better, it's healthier for you, and it is better for the community, local economy and the environment.

Local Okanagan produce is so amazingly fresh and you get inspired just looking at how beautiful the ingredients are. Jas says 'you feel healthy just looking at the produce'. The Okanagan has inspired us to use ingredients that aren't typically used in Indian dishes and create our own Indo-Okanagan twist.
The food industry has changed a lot throughout the years and you just don't know what's in your food anymore. That's why knowing where your food comes from is so important. With our local suppliers we're confident in how our raw ingredients are grown, raised and reared, and the products are just made with more love. It is a team effort, especially when you're working with a seasonal menu. You have to keep on communicating to see how the crops are doing and our suppliers are the experts in what they do – so they can give us suggestions too.
Okanagan cuisine can be anything, as long as it's made with Okanagan produce. Our homemade paneer and yoghurt is made using local milk. Our naan bread is made using local organic eggs. Our Ocean Wise seafood largely comes from Tofino and Haida Gwaii from Codfathers. Where possible we like to change our menu seasonally to make the most of what the Okanagan and BC has to offer."

THE FARMER
Wolfgang Wesle, Green Croft Gardens, Grindrod

At every Kelowna farmers' market, rain or shine, you will probably see owner/farmer Wolfgang Wesle standing under his Green Croft Gardens awning. Since 1988 Wolfgang and his wife Gabriele have owned and operated a 20 acre Certified Organic farm in Grindrod bordering the Shuswap River. A favorite supplier to local chefs and restaurants, Green Crofts sells also at local farmers' markets from Kelowna to Enderby.

The Wesle family is a true example of old world sustainability practice and they promote the locavorian philosophy. Wolf has a degree in Agriculture from Germany, with a background in dairy science. When he first moved to Canada he worked in the dairy industry for 15 years before focusing on vegetable growing. Green Croft Gardens is one of the earliest Certified Organic farms in the Okanagan. Wolf has found a change in consumer attitude towards shopping local. He believes that recently the awareness and growth of the local movement has been sparked by food shortage scares, and continued through the 100-mile diet movement. For the future, Wolf anticipates the joining of mainstream grocery stores in purchasing local organics as another way to connect local producers to local consumers.

Wolf is very active in mentoring young farmers and people interested in organic farming.

His science background is very evident in how he plans and considers all aspects of his farm. The amount of labor involved in weed management and thought required for soil management in order to sustain organic farming for the long term is incredible. As is the hours of labour he puts into the farm. Green Croft's mentorship and teaching philosophy has also led them to bring *WOOFERS on to the farm."

*World Wide Opportunities on Organic Farms www.wwoof.org

THE BREWMASTER
Ron & Patt Dyck, Cannery Brewing, Penticton

The Cannery Brewing Company in Penticton is one of many high quality local microbreweries that have been popping up around the valley. This all-natural craft brewery was opened in 2000 by Ron and Patt Dyck, former owners of Naramata's Country Squire Restaurant for 23 years. Brew Master Terry Schoffer joined the Dycks and they created the first batch of beer in Penticton's Old Alymer Fruit and Vegetable Cannery in 2001. In November 2010, the team celebrated their 1000th brew.

In her own words:
"The microbrew industry is flourishing. There is a market for all kinds of well-made and flavourful products. Beer is one of those products. We find that people from all walks of life, from all backgrounds, from all social groups, age groups and sexes are looking for great tasting beers. They are sometimes non-wine drinkers but most commonly they are wine, spirits and beer consumers who are interested in flavour and good value in a non-chemical beverage. It will just open everything up for breweries to produce more and different great beers.

Beer is actually easier to pair with many foods than wine is. Beer also lends itself to being cooked into great dishes. As people get used to trying lots of different styles of beer, they also get used to all of the different flavour combinations that this opens up."

PAIRING

Cannery Brewing India Pale Ale:

Hoppy and fun, this beer was brewed with a blending of four Pacific Northwest hop varieties. The rich malt flavours produce a complex character and lingering hop finish. "Although this beer has fierce hop, it will surprise with its gentle bite."

Main Courses

Braised Venison Shank w/ Roast Cipollini Onion & Thyme Bread Pudding

Chef: Grant de Montreuil, Bonfire Grill at The Cove, West Kelowna
Farmer: Richard Yntema, North Okanagan Game Meats, Enderby
Winemaker: Harry McWatters Collection

Venison is a delicious and extremely healthy meat choice. It is lean and hormone/antibiotic free. The deer raised on North Okanagan Game Meats Farm live in a beautiful, sunny pasture and enjoy a wonderful life. Although the shanks in this dish could be replaced with veal – I suggest giving venison a go. This dish would perfectly pair with a crisp autumn Okanagan day.

Serves 4
4 - 2" venison shanks (use hind leg shanks)
2 L brown venison stock, (can substitute beef stock)
1 L Okanagan Marechal Foch red wine
2 to 3 star anise pods
1 bay leaf
seasoned flour with salt, pepper and paprika
olive oil to coat pot

Dredge shanks in flour mix, then brown in oil in 4" deep pot or pan. Stock should completely cover meat. Add wine, star anise, bay leaf and stock. Bring to a boil and set in preheated oven at 350^0 - no lid. Let cook until stock has reduced and half of the meat is sticking out of the liquid - about 2 – 3 hours.
It should be deep dark brown in color and tender to the point of almost falling off the bone. Set aside.

Bread pudding:
8 cipollini onions, peeled and quartered
sprig of fresh thyme
olive oil, to coat pan
6 croissants
2 eggs
150 ml heavy cream
salt and pepper, to taste
pinch of nutmeg

Toss onions in oil with thyme leaves. Set in oven at 350ºF and roast until they become translucent and brown a little on the edges. Rip up croissants into small chunks, beat eggs and pour over croissants with cream. Add seasonings and onions. Using hands mix until well incorporated. Divide mixture into 4, 5oz ramekins that have been brushed with oil. Bake in 350^{0}F oven until golden brown.

Oregon Grape Compote
(start a couple of days ahead):
1 L Oregon grapes (Oregon grapes are found in abundance in the Okanagan)
500 g white sugar

In a bowl, mash the Oregon grapes with the sugar. Let rest in fridge for a couple of days to macerate. Strain juices into a small sauce pan and bring to a boil, let simmer for 5 minutes and skim any impurities off the top. Add mashed grapes and bring back to a boil for another 5 minutes, removing any impurities from the top. Pass through a fine mesh sieve. You won't get a lot of compote, as Oregon grapes are very seedy and dense, but the little you get will be worth the effort (YUM).

Chanterelle Mushroom Fricassee:
1 lb fresh chanterelle mushrooms*
1 leek, cleaned and diced
olive oil, to coat pan
4 fl oz Okanagan white wine
1 medium-sized tomato, skinned, seeded and diced
2 oz butter
salt and pepper to taste

Clean and slice mushrooms. In sautée pan on high heat add oil then leeks. Sweat leeks for a couple of minutes and add chanterelles, cook through. Add wine and sauté. Add cold butter and remove from heat, stirring rapidly to incorporate and create sauce. Season to taste.

Assembly:
Warm bread pudding and remove from ramekin – set on plate. Heap mushrooms beside bread pudding. Set venison shanks beside the other two items. Set pot back on stove and bring to a rapid boil; add a couple of ounces of cold butter to "mount" sauce. Serve drizzled atop.

You will find local chanterelle mushrooms in season at the farmers' markets and local fruit stands. Their extraordinary earthy flavour is prized by chefs and can be preserved in air free Ziplocs in the freezer – either sautéed first or not. Make sure to clean them with a brush or wiped with a damp paper towel. Trim ends and bad bits off first.

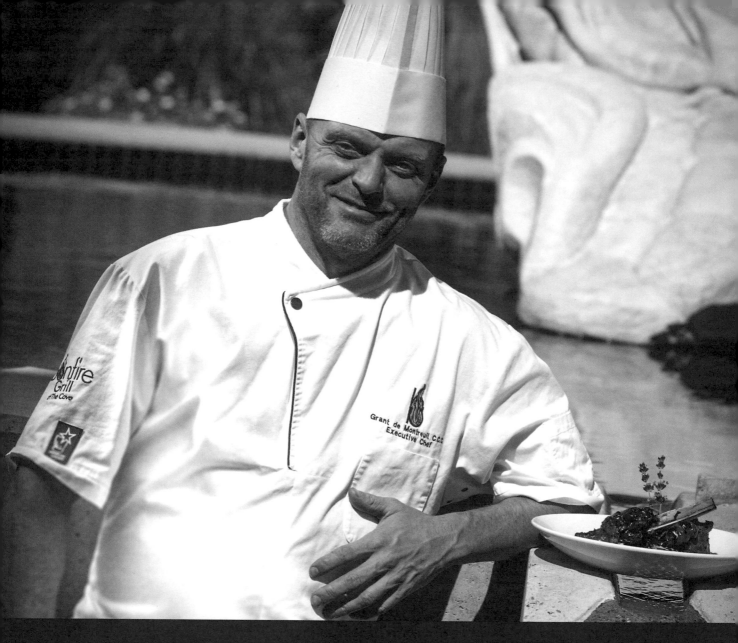

THE CHEF

Grant de Montreuil, Bonfire Grill at The Cove, West Kelowna

Born and raised in Kelowna, Chef de Montreuil was a pioneer in local, gourmet food with his restaurant de Montreuil's being THE local hot spot for diners in the 90's. He was also key in styling and creating menus for several local restaurants.

In his own words:
"I am a local product, and from a farming family, cooking locally is as much political as it is my passion. I have, over the years, set up numerous relationships with local growers, artisans and purveyors of meats and poultry. I first used the farm to folk co-op in Vancouver whilst learning my trade. Herb Barbolet at Glorious Garnish and Seasonal Salad Co. seemed to be speaking my language at the time as I was always left wondering why it was easier to get an apple from New Zealand or the US than it was to get one from my hometown Kelowna? From there I got in touch with Dale Zeich at Little Creek Gardens and from there it seemed to build steam under its own power."

THE FARMER

Richard Yntema, North Okanagan Game Meats, Enderby

Richard Yntema has become an iconic supplier to Okanagan chefs. Located in beautiful Enderby, Richard's Game Meats Farm and Valley Meats Abattoir, a more poetic name for slaughterhouse, are essential to the industry and to the future of ethical animal processing.

A house builder by trade, Richard and his family left their home in Abbotsford 22 years ago to come to the Okanagan and buy a farm. A friend directed him to a deer farm, his new home, where he dreamed of farming part time while continuing his trade. That never happened – Richard was a full time farmer from the start.

Richard's focus is to raise and source hard-to-find products for chefs across the valley. He raises wild boar, deer, lamb and chickens and sources other meats like rabbit, veal and exotic poultry to serve his customers.

In 2008 the government changed the licensing requirements for processing meat privately. This new law wreaked havoc on the farming industry, forcing farmers to transport livestock as far as the coast to a processing plant. This process was not only financially hard on the farmer, it was also hard on the animal.

Richard made a major investment in operations to become a provincially licensed processing plant and is now able to butcher his own livestock as well as others on the farm.

Richard is passionate and philosophical about his calling and works hard to keep things running. "I hope to pass this farm operation on to my kids as well as my passion to grow things."

Very much a part of our culinary education culture, chefs like Rod

Butters as well as the Culinary Arts Department at Okanagan College bring their team and students to Richard's farm for farm tours and to view the animal processing. Richard says the best chefs understand the "connection to the animal and to understand where the meat comes from." He also offers the peace of mind that the animals enjoyed "a good life on his farm." The wild boar roam freely in a mini forest area and the deer frolic in a beautiful pasture. Richard has set a high standard for animal farming as well as running a green operation. The entire operation is run on geothermal heating and cooling systems, making his carbon footprint zero.

THE WINEMAKER

Harry McWatters, McWatters Collection, Summerland

The McWatters philosophy: Sustainability is not a certificate, it is an attitude. The McWatters family is legendary in our food and wine world. Harry McWatters, who graciously wrote a foreword to this book, is known as a pioneer in our wine industry and to many as the godfather of the wine world. He has been growing grapes and making wine here for over 40 years and counts being founder of British Columbia's first estate winery, Sumac Ridge Estate Winery

in 1980 and founder of See Ya Later Ranch Estate Winery in 1995 as some of his many accomplishments. He is also the founder of the BC Wine Institute.

Richard "Dick" Cleave and Harry's daughter Christa-Lee McWatters-Bond (also co-owner of Local Lounge • Grille) are partners in this newest McWatters wine venture that focuses on wines that reflect the unique terroir of the Black Sage Bench.

PAIRING

2009 McWatters Collection Meritage

Although many people, including many wine experts, have a tendency to Frenchify the word "Meritage" by pronouncing its last syllable with a "zh" sound, as in "garage," the Meritage Alliance specifically states that the word should be pronounced to rhyme with "heritage." The grapes (Cabernet Sauvignon 44%, Merlot 32%, and Cabernet Franc 24%) were carefully selected at the peak of ripeness. The wine was then matured in small French oak casks for 15 months before bottling.

Rich and velvety, this Meritage is a luxurious wine. With notes of blackberry and dark chocolate and subtle hits of pepper, it pairs well with a romantic afternoon visit or a cozy Okanagan night.

DON'T WORRY, BRIE HAPPY OKANAGAN WRAP

CHEF: CHRIS ROWLAND & KELSEY GALT , BASKET CASE PICNICS, KELOWNA
FARMER: MIKE HAMBLETT, HAMBLETT HIGHLAND TURKEY FARM, SPALLUMCHEEN VALLEY
WINEMAKER: ANCIENT HILLS WINERY, KELOWNA

The Okanagan is picnic country. Rolling vineyards, lakeside beaches and wide open parks and even the ski hills in the winter just scream for a picnic date. Basket Case Picnics operates a buzzing food truck business, hopping around the valley from farmers' market to winery offering their delicious picnic meals packaged up and ready to go – just add wine and you have the perfect Okanagan experience.

Ingredients
1 bunch fresh spinach, washed
1 round of Brie (local suggestion: Mountain Meadow Sheep Milk Brie)
1 pkg. tortilla wraps (ancient grains or spinach variety work well)
1 bunch romaine leaves, washed
suggested accoutrements:
roasted garlic aioli (purchase or make)
caramelized onions

Roasted Cider Brined Turkey Breast with Peach Rosemary Glaze:
2 cups apple cider, plus 4 tbsp
1/4 cup salt, plus more for turkey
3 to 5 sprigs thyme
3 sprigs rosemary plus 1 tsp, chopped
1 boneless Hamblett turkey breast, skin on
1 cup onion, finely chopped
2 tbsp olive oil, plus more for turkey
freshly ground black pepper
2 lbs fresh (or 2, 10-ounce bags frozen) peeled and sliced peaches, chopped
4 tbsp honey
2 tsp Worcestershire sauce
2 tbsp brown sugar
1 tsp jalepeno pepper, seeds removed, fine dice
1 tsp Chinese 5-spice powder

Directions:
In a large bowl, whisk together 2 cups apple cider, salt, thyme and rosemary. Add turkey breast and enough water to cover the bird. Cover and let brine in the refrigerator 2 hours. Preheat oven to 425º F.

For the glaze:
In a small saucepan, sauté onions in oil until softened. Add peaches, honey, Worcestershire sauce, brown sugar and remaining 2 tablespoons apple cider. Bring to a boil. Lower to a simmer and cook until peaches break down and glaze thickens, about 12 minutes. Divide glaze mixture in half.

Remove turkey from brine and pat dry with paper towels. Brush with oil and season with pepper. Place turkey in a roasting pan. Cook 15 minutes until skin begins to turn golden. Reduce the oven temperature to 350ºF and brush the top generously with the glaze, reapplying every 15 minutes. Continue cooking until an instant-read thermometer inserted in the thickest part of the breast reaches an internal temperature of 165ºF, about 45 minutes. Let the turkey rest at least 10 minutes. Its temperature will continue to rise. To reserved half of glaze mixture, add diced jalapeno or other favorite hot pepper to desired heat level, and 1 teaspoon Chinese 5 spice powder, and additional peaches to thicken to 'chutney' consistency. Simmer until reduced to desired consistency. Set aside to cool.

Assemble the wrap:
Prepare wrap surface with roasted garlic aioli. Across the middle of the widest part of the wrap, place strips of Mountain Meadow Sheep Milk Brie, side by side, and almost the full width of the wrap. Top with peach 'chutney', and cover with caramelized onions. Season with salt and pepper and top generously with fresh washed and dried spinach leaves. Top with a large romaine leaf and roll and wrap! Great served fresh and cool, or with a light grilling Brie side down, to melt and meld flavors further.

HAMBLETT HIGHLAND FARM

LAPIN
Cherry
Box
Special
$45.00
18 pounds

Kelsey Galt

Chris Rowland (R)
with Mike Hamblett

THE CHEFS

Chris Rowland & Kelsey Galt, Basket Case Picnics, Kelowna

Basket Case Picnics actively promotes the 100-mile diet concept by incorporating the best in local, organic, and hormone-antibiotic free ingredients in its gourmet creations. The perfect addition to wine country, the Basket Case Picnic Street Food Truck parks at farmers' markets, wineries and events across the Valley.

In her own words:
"As a new generation caterer, we have embraced the gourmet street food craze! We actively engage with businesses in cross and co-promotion, ultimately offering local, healthy, high quality prepared foods for their clientele. For these businesses, especially picnic licensed vineyards, we are filling a distinct customer service void. Where they did not have the capacity, capital, or interest in adding a restaurant component to their existing profile, Basket Case Picnics steps in with the provision of fresh, restaurant quality products. Basket Case Picnics & Catering is resoundingly partnership and locally driven....that is why you will find us close to producers, serving à la carte from our mobile 'restaurant' at area farmers' markets, where we are featured like a 'demo kitchen' . We shop as close to exclusively with local producers as we can get, and evolve our menu to feature the best of what is in season from a wide range of local producers."

THE FARMER

Mike Hamblett, Hamblett Highland Turkey Farm, Spallumcheen Valley

The Hamblett Highland Turkey Farm is located between Vernon and Armstrong in the beautiful Spallumcheen Valley. If you have visited the Kelowna Farmers' & Crafters Market, you will remember Mike – he is the guy with the live turkey in a cage. (Mike assured us that the turkeys chosen as ambassadors to the public at the market are pardoned and become farm pets.)

Hamblett's turkeys are fresh, free run and are raised without hormones or medications.

In his own words:

"I started farming in 1993 in the Armstrong area. I had Certified Organic status and grew garlic. I had various types of poultry on a small scale including broiler chickens, laying hens, and turkeys. In 2003, I focused on turkey production and highland cattle.

I view farming as an exciting challenge to break away from commercial, conventional farming methods, to create a superior alternative for my local community. My turkeys are grown without any medication in their feed; they are raised out of doors, and grown much slower than commercial birds. This produces much better quality, and I think, healthier food.

I started researching other forms of feed, and found researchers back in the 30's and 40's were using feed sources such as fresh forage and alfalfa silage with good results. This would allow me to lessen my commercial feed usage and produce superior results with more natural local feed sources. Today's turkeys are very different from past breeds and it will require some time to perfect these practices. As well, I am working on developing a sustainable flock of heritage turkeys. They started hatching this summer. As you can see I am very much stepping back into the future.

Since I have been regularly attending the farmers market and offering turkey parts, the response has been really encouraging. People are now including this nutritious food in their diet on an ongoing basis. People appreciate that these products are available locally and are very enthusiastic to support local producers. My regular clients thank me all the time for providing this delicious food at the market."

THE WINEMAKER

Ancient Hills Winery, Kelowna

As their elegant label explains, "Earth, Air and Water inextricably combined, provide the platform for the eternal circle of life to play out." The Kamphuys family at Ancient Hill Winery pays tribute to the elements and unique history of our Okanagan soil that nourishes its vines and provides their fruit its unique and rich flavours.

Owner Richard Kamphuys chose the winery's name after delving deep into the history of his land. Perhaps a common viewpoint from one who was raised in Europe where ancient civilizations are apparent for all to see – he pondered, what was here before? Interestingly he uncovered the fact that approximately 10,000 years ago glacial Lake Penticton extended through the area, explaining the unique sand and river rock in the soil. Richard says Ancient Hill is "a reflection on the past" and a celebration of the present.

Richard, an economist by trade, and wife Jitske moved here from Holland 20 years ago and purchased the property in its original orchard state back in 2003. Once realizing that grapes were a better choice, they replanted with vines. Since then, their vineyard and winery have been a labour of love and vision for the future now realized. All of their wines are Estate grown with the wines hand planted by the couple with Baco Noir, Pinot Gris, Gewürztraminer, Lemberger, Zweigelt and Pinot Noir. Winemaker is Christine Leroux.

The tasting room will whisk you away to the majesty of Europe's castles and grand estates. The quality and craftsmanship are of the highest end, down to the 10x10 foot cellar doors – Ancient Hill weaves a rich tapestry of nature's gifts. Slate floors, stonework and reclaimed fir were used in the creation of the doors and the beautiful tasting bar - no detail was missed. The gardens were lovingly planted and maintained by Jitske who also played a large part in the decorative accents throughout the winery.

PAIRING

Ancient Hills 2009 Gewürztraminer

A bouquet of roses and lychee on the nose. Palate is crisp and fresh with a lovely spicy finish. This wine is the perfect date for a turkey.

Pan Seared Sterling Springs Chicken Scaloppini with Okanagan Berry Salsa, Roasted Fingerling Potatoes & Dill Kohlrabi Salad

CHEF: WILLI FRANZ, GRAPEVINE RESTAURANT AT GRAY MONK ESTATE WINERY, LAKE COUNTRY
FARMER: STERLING SPRINGS CHICKEN, FALKLAND
WINEMAKER: GRAY MONK ESTATE WINERY, LAKE COUNTRY

This recipe is a true celebration of the first harvests of the season. Berries arrive on the scene bursting with flavour and colour and the tender Fingerling potatoes, like digging for treasure, emerge from the soil like magic. Kohlrabi is a favorite vegetable for those with German heritage. Enjoy them raw, peeled straight from the garden for a tender, spicy treat that tastes similar to a cabbage heart, or cook them and enjoy in a salad like Chef Willi has demonstrated. (Kohlrabi comes from the German name for cabbage: kohl - kohlrabi or knol-khol is also known as a German turnip).

Ingredients:
8 thin slices (3oz. each) of Sterling Springs chicken breast, boneless & skinless
1 cup of blueberries /1 cup of strawberries / 1 cup of raspberries
3/4 cup of red onions, fine diced
2 garlic cloves, crushed
1/2 oz cilantro, chopped
1 tbsp vegetable honey
12 oz fingerling potatoes
two medium size kohlrabi
1/4 oz fresh dill, chopped
¼ tsp rosemary, chopped
1/2 cup of calamondin balsam vinegar*
grapeseed oil, salt, pepper, olive oil, white wine vinegar

*Calamondin is a citrus, also known as a Panama orange. The Balsam (vinegar) has intense flavour so use sparingly. This vinegar is available at Crescendo in Kelowna.

Okanagan Berry Salsa
Toss one cup of each Okanagan blueberries, strawberries, and raspberries and add 1/2 cup of red onion, 1/2 oz of finely chopped cilantro, two cloves of crushed garlic, 1 tbsp of Okanagan vegetable honey and a 1/4 cup of calamondin balsam vinegar. Salt and pepper to taste.

Roasted Fingerling Potatoes
Cut 12 oz of fingerling potatoes in half tossed with chopped rosemary and grapeseed oil in a bowl. Place on cookie sheet and roast in the oven at 380ºF for approximately 12 minutes.

Dill Kohlrabi Salad
Peel two medium-sized kohlrabi, cut into small sticks, and blanch in boiling water for 5 minutes, then place in ice water and cool. Place the kohlrabi in a bowl, add 1/4 cup of fine diced red onions, 3 tbsp olive oil, 1 tbsp of white wine vinegar. Salt and pepper to taste and finish with a 1/4 oz of fresh chopped dill.

Chicken Scaloppini
Sear the chicken scaloppini in a medium hot pan with 2 tbsp grapeseed oil for approximately 3 minutes on each side until done and set aside- keep warm.

To assemble plate:
Place roasted fingerling potatoes and dill kohlrabi salad on a plate, add two seared chicken scaloppini and top with the Okanagan berry salsa.

Willi Franz (L) and
Lisa Dueck

THE CHEF

Willi Franz, Grapevine Restaurant at Gray Monk Estate Winery, Lake Country

In his own words:
"I love being able to utilize all four seasons in my cooking style. Although trained in classical French cuisine, my style has evolved over the years and has led me to wine country cooking. I make it a priority to assemble the best seasonal local products and to pair them with delicious Gray Monk Estate wines.

I believe in the last 20 years Canada has, with its crop of young chefs created its own style of cooking. I believe Canadian cooking in the Okanagan is more local and very innovative. I would like to see everyone using more sustainable and renewable sources of food while always supporting our local growers and purveyors.

Okanagan cuisine is cooking with food products of the growing season when food is at its absolute best.

My suppliers are sourcing me as much as I'm sourcing them! I enjoy meeting them and discussing products, their availability and always support them as much as I can.

Operating a restaurant at Gray Monk Estate Winery makes the role of food and wine pairing very important. All our menu items are paired with Gray Monk Estate wines and I bridge the flavors of the wine with the flavors of the food."

THE FARMER
Sterling Springs Chicken, Falkland

Back when they were commercial farming, Hans and Lisa Dueck raised about 50,000 birds in an 8-week cycle on their farm. In 2011, they decided to reduce their operation, focusing on quality instead of quantity with a current quota from 65,000 birds per cycle to approximately 500 birds per cycle during summer months. This size allows the Duecks to focus on each bird, ensuring its high quality lifestyle and health, providing sustainably grown, medication-free chicken.

In her own words:
"The key to a great-tasting chicken is a stress-free life for the birds. Every factor, right down to the smallest detail, will affect (either positively or negatively) the taste and quality of the meat.

The benefits of local, sustainably raised, medication-free chicken are three-fold: (a) Consumers today are increasingly interested in how their food is being raised, what it's being fed, and how it's being treated. If they are able to establish a trust with a producer, to know that their food is being raised in a way they agree with, it results in a confidence and peace-of-mind about their food choices. (b) It's this simple: animals should be treated with respect. By virtue of the fact that they are living beings, they thrive with clean environments, nutritious food, and care. There are many farmers who provide this sort of environment for the animals in their care, and we support this philosophy whole-heartedly. (c) Local food typically does not travel as far as its counterparts, which can lower its carbon footprint. Also, raising chickens as sustainably as possible means that the chickens' needs are met, while fewer resources are needed to provide them with a clean, comfortable environment."

THE WINEMAKER
Gray Monk Estate Winery, Lake Country

2012 was a year of celebration for local winemaking pioneers owners George and Trudy Heiss of iconic Gray Monk Estate Winery in Kelowna: "30-40-50"- 30 years in operation, 40 years of grape growing and George and Trudy's 50th wedding anniversary.

In 1972 George and Trudy purchased an old orchard and converted it to a vineyard. They were at the front of the line presenting their request to be allowed to make (and sell) wine from their own grapes - this began the Estate Winery program - which many believe was the turning point for British Columbia Wines. 1976 marks a key moment in history when George decided to import vines from Europe. He planted 2,000 vines of Auxerrois, 50 of Pinot Gris and 10 of Gewürztraminer from a nursery in Alsace, giving vinifera a lasting foothold in the vineyard. The Pinot Gris became one of Gray Monk's signature wines. Following the training of George Heiss Junior as a winemaker in Germany, Gray Monk Estate Winery officially opened in 1982 - the winery

George and Trudy Heiss

was named for the grape variety Pinot Gris which in Austria is known as the Gray Monk.

In 2001 Gray Monk opened one of the first winery restaurants heralding the birth of the local wine country cuisine created by Chef Willi Franz.

PAIRING

2011 Gray Monk Pinot Gris

Pale gold in colour, this Alsatian style Pinot Gris has fresh apples and honey on the nose. The palate is smooth and ripe with hints of pineapple and lychee. Would work beautifully with spicy foods as well.

ORGANIC PEAS w/ RAINBOW TROUT & WILDFLOWER HONEY GLAZED PORK BELLY

CHEF: ROB CORDONIER, HILLSIDE WINERY BISTRO, PENTICTON
FARMER: TED & MAUREEN BROWN, TED'S TROUT, KAMLOOPS
WINEMAKER: HILLSIDE ESTATE WINERY, PENTICTON

Author's story: Trout is a quintessential Okanagan cuisine. I grew up trout fishing up at our family cabins at Minnow Lake and Oyama Lake and one of my favorite places in the world is the old cabin on Minnow Lake. My Grandpa Weisbeck and his pals built the cabin themselves in the early 1950's and I feel his spirit is still there. I have taken over shares in the cabin and relish the summer bookings when we can escape back in time to a place filled with special memories and a lake full of rainbow trout and singing loons. Over the years I have learned all of the family fishing tricks guaranteed to land you a pail full of trout. #1. Old Faithful – my Dad's fishing rod (purchased on my parents' honeymoon at The Army & Navy in Seattle 47 years ago.) #2. Opa's secret lure: corn, pea, corn. #3. Grandpa's secret fish call: "Heeeere fishy fishy…"

Wild Flower Honey Glazed Pork Belly:
2 lb wild boar belly (skin on) (or pork belly) (local suggestion: North Okanagan Game Meats)
2 tbsp vegetable oil
1 bottle Okanagan white wine
4 cups water
1 leek, sliced
1/8 cup fresh ginger, sliced
2 cloves garlic, sliced
1/2 cup rice vinegar
1 cup wildflower honey

It is best to prepare the pork belly the day before. Start by placing the pork in a medium heavy bottomed pot and submerging in cold water. Put the pot over high heat and bring to a simmer for 10 minutes. Remove the pork belly from the water and pat dry with kitchen towels. Discard the water and all the impurities from the pork. Clean the pot and put over medium - high heat add the vegetable oil. Place the pork skin side down in the pot and sear until the skin is golden brown. Turn the pork over and repeat the process on the other side. When the meat is well browned, add the rest of the ingredients and bring to a simmer. Cover the pot with a lid and put into the oven at 300ºF for 45 minutes. Turn the meat and replace the lid. Continue to braise for another 45 minutes or until very tender. Cool for 20 minutes in the cooking liquid. Remove the meat and press between two heavy dishes overnight in the fridge. Strain the sauce and reduce over low heat until it reaches a syrup consistency. Reserve the honey glaze until needed.

Summer Pea Salad:
1 cup sugar snap peas, sliced
1 fennel bulb, shaved
2 medium heirloom tomatoes, sliced
1 tbsp fresh chives, chopped
1 tbsp fresh basil, chopped
1 tsp lemon zest

3 tbsp extra virgin olive oil
1 tbsp white balsamic vinegar
pinch sea salt
pinch freshly ground pepper

It is best to make this salad fresh no more than 15 minutes before serving. Lightly mix all the ingredients together in a stainless steel bowl and taste for seasoning.

Trout:
4 fillets Ted's Chilcotin Rainbow Trout (pin bones removed, skin on)
2 tbsp vegetable oil
2 tbsp unsalted butter
sea salt as needed to season each fillet
organic pea shoots for garnish

Slice the pork belly into pieces approximately one centimeter thick. Sear over high heat on both sides until brown, turn the heat off and glaze with the reduced braising liquid and hold in a warm place until ready to plate. Place a large non-stick skillet over high heat and allow it to get hot. Season the trout fillets sparingly with sea salt. Add the oil to the pan and place the trout skin side down in the oil. Gently shake the pan to ensure the trout does not stick. Turn the heat down to medium-low and continue to cook until the skin is crispy and brown and the flesh is cooked about halfway through (approximately 90 seconds). Add the butter to the pan and gently turn the fish over onto the flesh. Once the butter starts to brown, remove the fish and place it onto paper towel to remove the excess cooking fat.

Divide the pea salad evenly among four plates and top with the fish and the pork belly. Garnish the plate with pea shoots and drizzle with the warm Wildflower Honey Glaze (local suggestion: Harker's Market, Cawston.)

TIP: If you don't have the opportunity to fish for your own trout, visit Jon Crofts at Kelowna's Codfathers Seafood Market; he carries Ted's Trout.

L-R: Chef Rob Cordonier, Winemaker Kathy Malone and Chef Brent Pillon

THE CHEF

Rob Cordonier, Executive Chef, Hillside Estate Winery Bistro, Naramata

Chef Cordonier spent the formative years of his career studying with some of British Columbia's most revered chefs and restaurant teams working in Vancouver and Whistler.

Wine eventually drew him to the Okanagan where he took on the position of Restaurant Chef at the Sonora Room Restaurant at Burrowing Owl Estate Winery. Chef Cordonier joined the Hillside team in 2010 and is enthusiastically pairing Hillside Estate wines with the bounty of the Okanagan fields in their Bistro.

In his own words:
"My mission at Hillside is to produce interesting flavor combinations to compliment our wines. We prepare our dishes simply and treat the ingredients with the utmost respect. Our local farmers are growing incredible produce that takes centre stage on our menu. It is their best that I take great pride in showcasing on your plate. We used to have suppliers delivering Okanagan produce to the restaurants I was working at in Vancouver - perfect peaches picked the day before, cherries the size of a toonie,

heirloom tomatoes that came in every color of the rainbow. Now I get to go to the farm and eat the peaches right off the tree. This growing region also has supported an incredibly diverse and ever expanding bouquet of grapes for local winemakers to manipulate into amazing wines. To be able to enjoy and pair a different wine from your own backyard every night is just magnificent. The food and the wine brought me here, but it is the contagious passion of the people who are a part of the food and beverage scene here in the Okanagan that have made this such a rich experience to be a part of as a chef. The food industry I feel is the key to really turning the region into a world class, year round destination. The chefs and farmers will continue to pursue our passions and grow together. Our winemakers are going to continue to perfect their craft and find new markets for their wines. I would really like to see it all eventually tied together with a school devoted to the arts of the table. We have everything here to be teaching a master class in organic farming, winemaking, vineyard management, cooking, baking, and be a destination for students as well as diners."

THE TROUT FARMER

Ted and Maureen Brown, Ted's Trout, Kamloops

L-R: Ted Brown, Jon Crofts and Maureen Brown at Codfathers in Kelowna.

Located near Little Fort, BC, Ted and Maureen Brown run a small family-operated trout farm that has been providing locally grown Kamloops Rainbow Trout since 1985. Ted's happy trout have also been stocked abundantly in many small private lakes and ponds throughout the province.

In their own words:

"Ted and I got the opportunity to take over the existing farm from a retiring couple in 1985. (We had been travelling in Australia and southeast Asia and came home to Canada to this wonderful offer from friends.)

Farming trout is a sustainable practice and boasts a 'green circle' (recommended to consumers of seafood and fish) by organizations such as OceanWise. It reduces impact on wild stock, and provides the general public with access to a high quality, sustainably-grown, local product. While we will never fully replace industrialized agriculture, eating locally ensures and supports the continued existence of local farms, heightens food security, and offers a viable and healthy alternative to outsourced food growing practices.

Selling our product is a necessary part of growing food, and restaurants require a high quality, consistent product, and are therefore a natural target for direct marketing. Chefs who do focus on local suppliers seem to value the relationships that it offers and realize quickly that generally the quality of food is higher.

Regarding the future of farming, we feel that on the one hand, many farms are disappearing, but on the positive side, society and consumers in general are experiencing increased awareness of where their food comes from; more and more people are caring about environmental issues, and seeing beyond their own immediate desires to a bigger, global picture, and therefore are more committed to supporting local farmers."

THE WINEMAKER

Hillside Estate Winery, Penticton

Chef Rob Cordonier works closely with Winemaker Kathy Malone to find the "soul of each wine" to build his cuisine around.

Kathy explains, "When I was considering the move to Hillside Estate Winery from Mission Hill Estate Winery, I thought these people were insane, planting Malbec this far north in the valley, I knew how hard it was to ripen Bordeaux varieties, even as far south as Osoyoos. But I tasted the wines and was impressed. . . confused, but impressed. Spending the summer of 2009 on the Naramata Bench, I got a sense of how we were able to achieve this level of ripeness. The Naramata Bench, having a west-facing aspect, enjoys the latest sunlight possible in the evening, before the sun dips down below the mountain. During these late afternoon hours, the sun reflects across the lake, bathing the vineyards in sunlight from below. This gives a doubling effect of photosynthesis and warms the soil. While their tannin structure is more elegant and refined than those of some "hot-pocket" reds, the flavour profiles of these wines exhibit complete ripeness, with well-balanced alcohols and acidity."

PAIRING

2011 Hillside Estate Winery Rosé

This Rosé is a blend of Merlot, Cabernet Franc, Gamay, and Pinot Noir. Deep rose in colour, it offers up bright aromas of rhubarb and red berries. The berries carry through to the palate with a crisp snap of citrus that awakens the taste buds. A perfect pairing for salmon.

OKANAGAN'S FINEST ROASTED PETITE TENDER "LE PETITE CLOS" WITH BLACK CURRANT GLACE DE VIANDE

CHEF: DUSTIN VINCENT, SONORA ROOM RESTAURANT, BURROWING OWL WINERY, OLIVER
FARMER: CAROLYN TIPLER, LE PETIT CLOS, OLIVER
WINEMAKER: BURROWING OWL ESTATE WINERY, OLIVER

Petite tender is a muscle from the shoulder chuck. While being extremely tender, the muscle is not often used due to requiring skill to extract it so beef tenderloin can be substituted in this recipe. Marinating the tender overnight really helps bring out the amazing beef flavor and the addition of Okanagan red wine marries the meat together with the currants beautifully.

Petite Tender or Beef Tenderloin (local suggestion: L&D Meats, Kelowna - tell Don the number of people you are serving and he will provide the right amount)

Marinade:
5-10 peppercorns
4 sprigs of thyme
3 bay leaves
500ml of Okanagan Merlot (local suggestion: Burrowing Owl Winery)
2 large shallots, sliced
3 cloves of garlic, sliced
4 juniper berries

Marinate in a zip lock bag for easy storage for 12- 24 hours. Pan roasting is the easiest method but barbequing would work just as well. Cook to your liking.

Black Currant Glace de Viande:
Chef Note: Making your own stock can be time consuming but also extremely rewarding for the end product.
A home sized recipe for stock:
4-5 veal bones
2 onions
3 stalks of celery
2 carrots
2 leeks (white only)
3-4 ounces tomato paste
5 garlic cloves
4 sprigs of thyme
2 sprigs rosemary
10 black peppercorns
3 bay leaves

Roast the veal bones in a 350ºF oven until browned (about 1.5 - 2 hrs.) Rub the tomato paste on the bones and allow to roast for 15 minutes more. Carefully move all the bones to your largest stock pot. Using the same tray roast all of your vegetables and garlic until well caramelized. Add all ingredients to your stock pot and put water to cover; slowly simmer the contents for 6-8 hours, then strain. In a clean stock pot, large enough to hold your veal stock, put 1 litre of red wine and reduce by half. Add your veal stock and turn to a medium simmer.
(Chef Note: Reducing this mixture of wine and veal stock by half would give you demi-glace; we are going to reduce this by 90%! So if you had 10 litres of stock you should have 1 litre of sauce remaining.)
At this point add 500ml of fresh black currants (Local suggestion: Le Petite Clos). Adding the black currants at the end will add sweetness to the Glace de Viande and they will retain a lot of their fruit flavor.

Chef's suggested sides to serve:
Confit Fingerling Potatoes:
Place in a pot with enough duck fat (olive oil for a healthier option) to cover. Add some aromatics, 4-6 peppercorns, 2 sprigs thyme and rosemary, 2 bay leaves, 2 sliced shallots and 2 fresh garlic cloves. On a low simmer cook the potatoes "al dente" just until a knife can pierce them. Cool them in the duck fat. Reheat to order in a sauté pan until nice and golden and warm throughout.

Carrots:
Poach them in a local organic apple cider for some sweetness on the plate while adding a bit of sour to break up some of the fat taste in the mouth.

Baby Patty Pan Squash:
Pan sear the baby patty squash until nice and golden, then finish with a bit of butter in the pan and allowing it to go "beurre noisette" (brown butter) – this provides an amazing nuttiness to the dish.

Beets:
Slow roasting unpeeled beets in the oven. Peel while warm for the easiest results. Oven roasting the beets really allows the sugars to come out. Toss with some olive oil and some finishing salt.

Local suggestions: Duck fat - Tony's Meats, Penticton; Mission Meats, Valaroso Foods Kelowna.

Sous Chef Dustin Vincent (L) with Carolyn Tipler

THE CHEF

Dustin Vincent, Sous Chef, Sonora Room Restaurant, Burrowing Owl Estate Winery, Oliver

Formerly working under Executive Chef Chris von Hooydonk at the Sonora Room, Dustin has enjoyed a great career at Burrowing Owl.

In his own words:
"Personally I was inspired to cook locally when I started meeting the local growers. What inspires me to cook with local food farms is working with the local people who are completely in love with their own product .
Some of these thoughts really go to show how we make our Okanagan food unique. We are part of the Sonoran Desert; our climate not only dictates what we can grow here, but it allows us to grow a lot of things great! The soil we plant our crops in and the water we use to grow them all make a difference; from the east side of the valley to the west side of the valley all of these little differences start adding up to how different and how great our product really is. Our true difference, the true aspect I think that really makes us unique, is the people that grow the food, the farmers that produce the local product. This is what I truly appreciate in our Okanagan Valley; without these people we would not have some of the best product in the world, but with them we do!"

THE FARMER

Carolyn Tipler & Francois Martel, Le Petit Clos, Oliver

In her own words:

"I have lived in the Okanagan/Shuswap since 1967 and retired from fulltime work in office management in 1999 when I moved to Oliver. In 2008 the decision was made to plant a bigger vineyard as the number of horses had decreased and it would provide some income. My partner Francois Martel had experience in viticulture and the vineyard is truly his domain. Le Petit Clos has been operating now for three years.

We are certified naturally grown for many reasons. Firstly we want to farm in a sustainable way, doing no harm and always putting back into the soil. Secondly we do not believe in chemical intervention for weed and pest control or for nutrition of plants. It can all be taken care of with good management. Thirdly we believe strongly in locally grown food, particularly in our beautiful valley where for the most part we have ideal conditions. British Columbia should be able to produce enough food for its population and right now it doesn't. That needs to change – food sovereignty is so important.

For the future I hope that more young people will be drawn into agriculture and that this will be encouraged by programs that make this possible.

You have to really love what you do, be passionate about farming as it is hard work and we are always at the mercy of weather – this year is a prime example. I wish I could have started this 20 years ago and hope that 20 years from now I still have my hands in the dirt!"

THE WINEMAKER

Burrowing Owl Estate Winery, Oliver

This legendary estate on Oliver's famous Golden Mile appears like a mirage over the desert's miles and miles of grapevines. The Wyse family built Burrowing Owl in 1998 after sourcing this unique eco-system in Oliver that is actually located on northernmost tip of the Sonoran Desert. Senior Winemaker Bertus Albertyn concentrates on four grape varietals from the 16 varieties grown at Burrowing Owl Vineyards.

The Burrowing Owl's Sonora Room Restaurant and beautiful accommodations have made this winery a top destination in wine country.

Winemaker Bertus Albertyn

PAIRING

2009 Burrowing Owl Syrah

This powerhouse wine is loaded with notes of rich berries and dark fruits with a spicy edge. It hits your palate with layers of flavours including chocolate, coffee and hints of vanilla. Beautiful lingering finish.

Root Vegetable Torte

CHEF: ROD BUTTERS, OWNER/CHEF RauDZ REGIONAL TABLE, KELOWNA
FARMER: JON AND SHER ALCOCK, SUNSHINE FARM, KELOWNA
WINEMAKER : MEYER FAMILY VINEYARDS, OKANAGAN FALLS

The Okanagan grows a plethora of root vegetables that harvest deep into fall allowing for high quality cellaring throughout the winter. Hearty and rich in flavour and vitamins these earthy vegetables represent a lifeline for local sustainable eaters who like to shop and eat by season. Chef Butters has dressed them up and presented them in all of their glory in this beautiful, vegetarian dish. Vegetables are care of his friends, Jon and Sher Alcock of Sunshine Farm.

Serves 4-6 people

Require 8" x 8" deep oven proof casserole dish
Mandolin (Japanese) if available.

Ingredients:
3 cloves garlic, minced
3 large shallots, sliced thin
1/2 cup shredded Parmesan
1 cup heavy cream
1/4 cup fresh herbs chopped (i.e.- parsley, rosemary, thyme, oregano - earthy flavoured herbs)

*All vegetables to be peeled and sliced as thin as possible using mandolin or knife.

2 large carrots
2 large beets- red &/or gold
1 medium rutabaga
2 medium white turnips
6 sunchokes (if available)
1 small celery root
2 medium parsnips
2 russet potatoes

3 oz mild goat cheese (local suggestion: Carmelis Goat Cheese Artisans)
sea salt and cracked black pepper

Method:
Pre-heat oven to 400˚ F.
Spray casserole dish with non-stick spray or line entire dish with parchment paper. (*if wanting to remove from pan for pre-slicing parchment paper will help in the removal of the torte from dish.)
Layer one variety of vegetable at a time in dish and between each layer sprinkle with garlic, shallots,

Parmesan, cream, herbs, salt and pepper.
Continue to alternate vegetables until casserole dish is full. Try alternating different colours of vegetables for the greatest effect. Sprinkle goat cheese on top layer. Cover very loosely with tin foil or parchment paper. Bake at 400ºF for approx 50-60 minutes or until center of casserole feels tender by inserting fork. A baking sheet can be placed under casserole dish just in case liquid escapes while baking. Remove from oven and let stand.
This torte can be served directly from the pan. Garnish with fresh seasonal greens and serve with Quadra Island scallops (also delicious on its own).

Chef Notes:
Casserole can be cooked day before and chilled. The Root Vegetable Torte can then be removed from dish, sliced and reheated as in photo.
This recipe can be adapted without using cream or cheese. Substitute a non- salted vegetable stock in place of cream.

(L-R) Jon Alcock (Sunshine Farm), Gerry Jobe (RauDZ Liquid Chef) and Chef Rod Butters.

THE CHEF

Rod Butters, Chef/Owner RauDZ Regional Table, Kelowna

Rod Butters opened the world famous Wickaninnish Inn, Tofino as Chef de Cuisine in 1996 helping the Inn's Pointe Restaurant attain the internationally recognized Relais & Chateaux designation.

In 2000, he moved to Kelowna to share his culinary experiences and open Fresco Restaurant & Lounge in Kelowna as Chef /Proprietor. One of the pioneer locavorian chefs, Rod has always been committed to serving regional cuisine. A visit to his current restaurant RauDZ Regional Table (co-owned with business partner Audrey Surrao) will testify to that – the walls are lined with photos of his suppliers.

In his own words:

"After five years in Tofino it was time for some sun! It was really the opportunity to live and work in an area that embraced my core values of supporting local. Eleven years ago there was not much here. Grant de Montreuil and Jim Armstrong (Harvest Golf Club) was about it.

The Okanagan is the chef's ultimate playground!!! Need I say more? It's all here right in our backyard – it doesn't get any better.

The future of our culinary scene here is very bright. We have a very active and supportive Chefs Association that is making positive changes within our community. There

are more highly trained chefs/cooks/servers/sommeliers moving here. This is a good indication as to the positive nature of our 'scene'.

I would like to see more independent restaurants/ businesses being supported by the community and a Hospitality Centre of Excellence is needed with a chef program, service, business, wine studies etc. We are also ready for a Relais & Chateaux type property or equivalent. i.e. Wickaninnish Inn, Sooke Harbor House, Langdon Hall. I feel our accommodation sector needs to catch up now. "Okanagan cuisine" is varied. Some chefs utilize global influences for example. For me, I try to stay true to my philosophy. The basis though, is and should be, in supporting local first. This includes ingredients, events, businesses, hiring practices....

My suppliers inspire me! Without them, we would just be 'another' restaurant. They are part of our team. Like Sunshine Farm - I originally met John and Sher Alcock's brother Doug to do some metal sculptures for Fresco (my former restaurant). Doug is quite a renowned metal artist. He introduced me and the rest is history. Jon and Sher have been with us since day 1. Their passion, knowledge, and friendship have been invaluable these past 11 1/2 years. Their daughter Mona and I even shot a pilot for a cooking show many years ago. They are not just farmers/ suppliers, they are family."

THE FARMER

Jon & Sher Alcock, Sunshine Farm, Kelowna

Jon and Sher Alcock and their son Russ operate Sunshine Farm nestled in South Kelowna. Their daughter Mona, a chef, participates in special farm events and dinners. Sunshine Farm includes a Certified Organic vegetable and herb garden with a forest of pine and fir with marsh meadows, mowland and a small heritage apple orchard. The majority of their food crop and seed production is of Certified Organic heritage or heirloom varieties, particularly Certified Organic tomatoes. The Alcocks have an organic seed catalog available on their website: www.sunshinefarm.net

In his own words:

"We started saving seeds really from the time we started farming, interested in some of the tomato varieties from some of our previous generation, growing and saving seed out of thrift to cut the seed bills in coming years and to ensure that we could get the varieties we wanted. The thing is, it became apparent that the number of varieties in the more common seedhouse catalogues were declining. We have selected several varieties and grown them to perform well in our Okanagan bio region, as they acclimatize to our hot summers, wet Junes and usually dry autumns.

We believe that it is important to preserve the genetics of past generations… literally thousands of years of plant breeding and selection and not allow them to be lost because the seed corporations see profit as the prime motivator in seed production. Most seeds commercially produced and sold currently are for hybrid varieties, those which will ripen all at once, can handle being mechanically harvested, and will sit on the supermarket shelf for weeks and taste nothing like the vegetable it is supposed to represent. No wonder kids don't like their vegetables - the supermarket varieties are tasteless, they don't really represent 'fruits of the land', they are of some other land and not grown in fertile living soil, they are grown industrially, and virtually

> *I kind of believe what the American philosopher/farmer Wendell Berry said, vaguely: that we are only really nourished by the plants and animals that are growing in the same soil as us.*

hydroponically with water and chemicals with the soil only as a growing medium.

We have been working since we arrived here at Sunshine Farm 25 years ago to build our soil, to nurture it as we would our crops for it is our greatest resource. We are located on the old beach front of Lake Penticton from about 12,000 years ago; our mineral soil is classified as 'Oyama Sandy Loam' and will grow anything with the right amount of water and organic matter incorporated into it. Our soil is able to coalesce the elements of seed, water, and sunshine to produce what some of our favorite chefs have called a unique, interesting and delicious terroir. They were talking about flavours of tomatoes and carrots - not grapes/wine as an expression of the land.

These are the sorts of encouragement from friends and chefs that have spurred us on to continue to produce these heritage varieties that are able to truly form an expression of the land through their flavour, form and function (nutrition)."

Sher Alcock with son Russell, Farm Manager

JAK Meyer (L) and
Chris Carson

THE WINEMAKER

Meyer Family Vineyards, Okanagan Falls

Wine critics love Meyer wines. This Burgundian focused winery has vineyards in both Naramata and Okanagan Falls and produces award-winning Chardonnays and Pinot Noirs.

Owners JAK Meyer and his wife Janice Stevens purchased a small vineyard in 2006 on the Naramata Bench and then two years later bought another in Okanagan Falls. Born and raised in Alberta, the Meyers were excited for the lifestyle change and ready to dive into the winery world.

Producing single vineyard wines, the wines are an excellent example of how terroir affects the expression of varietal character. They produce less than 3000 cases from mature 14-year-old vines. Winemaker Chris Carson is a graduate of Lincoln University, Canterbury, New Zealand with his Bachelor of Viticulture and Oenology. His traditional training focuses on hand-crafting Meyer's classic wines to display the unique characteristics derived from this Okanagan Valley terroir. Chris, after spending eight years in New Zealand where he worked with many prestigious wineries, also spent time in the famous Chassagne Montrachet region in Burgundy.

PAIRING

2010 Meyer Tribute Series Sonia Gaudet Chardonnay

This Chardonnay serves up notes of toasted brioche, hints of tropical fruit like grilled pineapple with ripe pears and has a long, lingering finish. It is a gorgeous example of Chardonnay at its best.

SEZMU BEEF TARTARE, WHIPPED DIJON CREAM, TOMATO BRIOCHE, MISSION HILL PICKLES

CHEF: MATTHEW BATEY, THE TERRACE RESTAURANT, MISSION HILL WINERY, WEST KELOWNA
FARMER: BILL AND DARLENE FREDING, SEZMU BEEF/OKANAGAN'S FINEST ANGUS BEEF, OLIVER
WINEMAKER: MISSION HILL FAMILY ESTATE WINERY, WEST KELOWNA

This beautiful dish makes for an elegant starter or light main course. Beef tartare is as common to menus in Paris as burgers are here. Using the highest quality beef available is key – and here we are fortunate to now find local beef. The lucky cows at Okanagan's Finest Angus Beef are served a glass or two of red with their meals, making them not only chic but delicious as well.

Beef Tartare:
250g Okanagan's Finest Angus Beef, hand chopped fine
1 tbsp brandy
1 tbsp shallots – *brunoise
1 tbsp pickles – *brunoise
1 tbsp capers – chopped fine
to taste Dijon mustard
to taste salt and pepper

Mix all ingredients and adjust seasoning if necessary.

Dijon Cream:
1 cup cream 35%
1 1/2 tbsp Dijon mustard
1 gelatin sheet
2 egg whites

Bloom gelatin in ice water. Simmer cream and mustard, add gelatin and allow to cool, and then add egg white. Transfer to **CO_2 container and reserve in an ice bath in the fridge.

Tomato Brioche:
batter – mix together:
280g milk
44g yeast
180 g all-purpose flour

Mix in:
550 g eggs
720 g all purpose flour
46 g sugar
12 g salt

Add last:
630g butter – soft
60g tomato paste

Mix. Allow dough to rest and set up overnight. Portion dough into 250g balls, roll out dough and place in a greased mould. Allow to proof for 20 – 30 minutes. Bake at 185º Celsius for 12 – 15 minutes.

Serve with:
pickles
Parmesan cheese
quail egg – sunny side up

*Brunoise is a culinary knife cut in which the food item is first julienned and then turned a quarter turn and diced again, producing cubes of a side length of about 3 mm or less on each side or 1/6 inch cubes.
**A CO_2 container, also known as a syphon, whipped cream dispenser, ISI whipper, is a pressurized container used to create culinary foams, whips etc.

The Chef

Matthew Batey, Executive Winery Chef, The Terrace Restaurant,
Mission Hill Estate Winery, West Kelowna

Matthew graduated with honours from Spectrum Community School in Victoria in 1997. A year later, he completed the Culinary Arts Program at Malaspina University College and was awarded the Instructors' Gold Medal. Matthew has been instrumental in defining the concept of "Cuisine du Terroir" – wine country cooking featuring locally-grown, in-season ingredients.

In his own words:
"What inspires me to cook locally? The fact that this is where we live, this is where my wife and I raise our family and the sheer nature of just how good the products are here.

The farmers, producers, artisans, cheese makers hands down work harder than we do, which is clearly a big statement. They are the cornerstone to our success; without their hard work and dedication to their craft, I wouldn't have a craft to practice. We have developed relationships over the years; frankly before it became vogue to cook locally. We want to ensure there is a portion of stability that is part of the relationship. We invest a lot to get us to the place where it works for both the producer and our team that we want to ensure the relationship is a long term one. It is an investment that pays dividends. You can't be choosy, only taking a little of this and that, a couple of times, we support the producers and in turn they give us the best their operation has to offer. We are really very fortunate with how good the products are that arrive into our kitchens. I think sometimes we forget that not all that is grown is perfect though, so I am glad that there are organizations in the valley like the food banks and the Gleaners who put the 'less' perfect products to good use.

We worked with Troy and Janice who were the original owners of the Sezmu brand. They approached us looking for insight into what the chef would want re cuts, specs and quality levels. Okanagan cuisine is real, honest and true to the producers."

THE FARMER

Bill and Darlene Freding, Sezmu Beef/ Okanagan's Finest Angus Beef, Oliver

The ultimate in wine country beef, these local cows are actually fed red wine! Sezmu cattle, now owned by Bill and Darlene Freding of Okanagan's Finest Angus Beef, are raised at Southern Plus Feedlot in Oliver where the cows are served one litre (that's 1.0568 U.S. quarts) of red wine each day during finishing. The red wine actually comes from the Freding's vineyards – they also make wine under the Rafter F label.

Bill and "Dar" firmly believe in the gentle, humane handling of their cattle resulting in healthy cows with few illnesses and need for medication. Their cattle are hormone and antibiotic free. Dar has even been known to bring a calf into their home to nurse if necessary. "We truly believe we own nothing, but we are the caretakers for the generations to come," says Bill Freding.

Okanagan's Finest Angus Beef carries the Certified BC Beef logo ensuring that the beef has been born, raised and processed in BC. The by-product (manure) of their cattle also provides and opportunity to play a role in ensuring that the agricultural lands of the South Okanagan have high quality compost that reduces water usage.

Temple Grandin's livestock practices have been used at Southern Plus for close to 20 years in order to minimize stress, ensure healthy animals and produce better beef.

*Temple Grandin (born August 29, 1947) is an American doctor of animal science and professor at Colorado State University, bestselling author, and consultant to the livestock industry on animal behavior. As a person with high-functioning autism, Grandin is also noted for her work in autism advocacy and is the inventor of the squeeze machine, designed to calm hypersensitive people.

The subject of an award-winning biographical film, Temple Grandin, in 2010, was listed in the Time 100 list of the 100 most influential people in the world in the "Heroes" category.

THE WINEMAKER

Mission Hill Family Estate Winery, West Kelowna

Mission Hill Family Estate Winery was originally established in 1966. Current owner Anthony von Mandl purchased it in 1981 and transformed the estate into a stunning and dramatic European style stone work of art including a landmark 85 foot high bell tower. Gazing down through rows of grapevines onto the majesty of our Lake Okanagan while dining al fresco at The Terrace Restaurant offers a quintessential Okanagan experience. Open seasonally, it is a must to experience.

John Simes (pictured right) is Head Winemaker at Mission Hill and creates wines across four tiers. Michel Rolland, a prominent French oenologist, has been consulting at the estate since 2005.

PAIRING

2010 Martin's Lane Pinot Noir

Named for Mission Hill Proprietor Anthony von Mandl's late father, Dr. Martin von Mandl, these Pinot grapes were hand-picked from select soils and vineyard parcels in Mission Hill's East and West Kelowna estates. A luscious berry bomb, enjoy notes of spice and concentrated blackberries that will merrily dance on your palate.

Slow Cooked Halibut w/ Basil, Crisp Sweet Life Farms Potatoes, Stoney Paradise Tomatoes, Artichoke and Chardonnay Emulsion

CHEF MARK FILATOW, OWNER/CHEF, WATERFRONT RESTAURANT & WINE BAR, KELOWNA
FARMER: STONEY PARADISE FARMS, KELOWNA
WINEMAKER: CHURCH & STATE WINERY, OLIVER

Fresh West Coast halibut season runs from March until early November. This beautiful white fish, that is actually extremely ugly in person, when cooked right is moist and buttery. Chef Filatow's version is a gorgeous example of this fish's grand potential. Make note of the cooking tips he shares – who knew that leaving cooked potatoes in the fridge uncovered over night aids in their crispiness? Thanks, Chef!

Serves 4

Potatoes (the day before):
4 russet potatoes (local suggestion: Sweet Life Farms)
sea salt

Peel and dice potato. Bring 2 litres of water to a boil.
Add 1 tbsp of salt to the water. Add potatoes.
Cook until almost falling apart.
Drain potatoes. On a plate lined with paper towel, refrigerate overnight uncovered! Can be done the same day but they won't be as crispy.
Deep fry potatoes with 2 litres oil in a pot at 350°F (or a deep fryer)

Artichoke Sauce:
100ml lemon juice
100ml Chardonnay (oaky version - local suggestion: Church & State Chardonnay)
100ml olive oil
100g cleaned fresh artichoke

Combine all in a pot and simmer on low with a lid on until the artichoke is tender. Approx. 15 minutes.
Blenderize and strain, season with salt to taste.
Reserve (can be made a day ahead).

Halibut:
200g Sungold cherry tomatoes (local suggestion: Stoney Paradise tomatoes)
halibut - 150g per person (or 5oz)
4 slices white onion
4 large basil leaves
olive oil
sea salt
On a large piece of tinfoil, coat the halibut with olive oil. Sprinkle generously with salt. Lay an onion slice down, place halibut on top, finish with a basil leaf. Repeat with the other 3. Place the halibut side by side and fold the foil over the fish, making a tight package. Place halibut in a 300°F BBQ onion side down for 10 minutes.

To Serve:
Slice tomatoes in half. Gently heat sauce. Place potatoes in oil until golden brown, remove from oil with a slotted spoon, place in a bowl and toss with tomatoes, add a little salt and pepper to taste. Divide potatoes on to four plates, place a piece of halibut on the potatoes, and include the juices from the tinfoil package. Ladle sauce around, garnish with more fresh basil. Serve!

THE CHEF

Mark Filatow,
Executive Chef/Owner
Waterfront Restaurant &
Wine Bar, Kelowna

With over 20 years of experience, Mark Filatow represents the pinnacle of culinary excellence and is the driving force behind Waterfront Restaurant & Wine Bar. After graduating with honours from the Dubrulle Culinary Institute, Mark honed his culinary skills at some of the most prestigious restaurants in BC including Tofino's Wickaninnish Inn, Vancouver's Bishops and Diva at the Met and Kelowna's Fresco Restaurant (now RauDZ Regional Table).

In 2001 Mark was accepted into the coveted Sommelier Guild, making him one of the only chefs in Canada with this level of skill in food and wine pairing.

In his own words:

What brought you to the Okanagan: "The lifestyle and ingredients, opening a restaurant. Summed up like this, being able to ride my bike into work, picking up some fantastic produce along the way and quenching my thirst with a glass of something local after work of course."

What makes Okanagan cuisine so unique? "The quality and freshness of our ingredients and how close the 'farm' is to the table. True 'Okanagan cuisine' is anything and everything that incorporates our local foodstuffs. Be it Indian, Japanese or French."

What would you like to see in our culinary future? "I would like to see more animal husbandry. More local proteins grown here."

What is your relationship like with your farmers/artisans? "I know the suppliers all by first name. I am eager to promote their products with other restaurants."

THE FARMER

Milan Djordjevich,
Stoney Paradise Farms, Kelowna

Chef Filatow describes his relationship with Milan, "I was working at Bishop's Restaurant in Vancouver when I met Milan (Stoney Paradise Farms) five years before I moved up to the Okanagan. He is the original 'Tomato Man'. His tomatoes are selected/picked for flavour. The farm is aptly named Stoney Paradise. The tomatoes struggle and produce amazing flavours. Sungolds are like tomato candy."

Stoney Paradise is literally a rock star of the tomato world. For years, Chefs from all over the province covet these special, old world tomatoes and feature them on menus from Bishop's Restaurant in Vancouver to Waterfront Restaurant & Wine Bar in Kelowna. Meticulous in his growing philosophies and care of his crops, Milan's tomato manifesto remains: "Tomatoes should be ripened on the vine, outside". Therefore these jeweled treasures are transported, farm to chef's table with extreme care at the perfect level of ripeness and flavour. An architect by training, Djordjevich began his devoted foray into the world of heirloom tomatoes 15 years ago and continues to maintain his trusted brand as The Tomato Man.

THE WINEMAKER

Church & State Wines, Oliver

Proprietor Kim Pullen

Church & State Wines opened up a second winery in Oliver in 2011, the first being in Brentwood Bay, Victoria. Kim Pullen, Proprietor of Church & State explains "To me the name of Church & State is that balance. To find a resting place between the vision of the heart and the practicality of the head. In Oliver we farm 60 acres on estate land, and a further 30 acres through our partnerships with growers in the Okanagan and Similkameen Valleys. We also have 11 acres of planted grapes on the Saanich Peninsula." The expertise of Winemaker Jeff Del Nin has been bringing in consistent accolades for their wines.

PAIRING

2010 Church & State Chardonnay

This Chardonnay is stunning. Sunlit hued and beautifully balanced, it offers a full buttery, mouthfeel. An elegant explosion of Okanagan stone fruits mingle with notes of vanilla on the nose that follow through to the palate. Pairs well with life.

Smoked BBQ Pork "Carnitas" Apple & Lime slaw - Pinto Bean

CHEF: STUART KLASSEN, DELTA GRAND OKANAGAN RESORT & CONFERENCE CENTRE, KELOWNA / PRESIDENT OKANAGAN CHEFS ASSOCIATION
FARMER: GLENN AND LORETTA CROSS, FUNCTION JUNCTION, KELOWNA
CIDERY: DOUBLE CROSS APPLE CIDERY, KELOWNA

Party size! 12- 15 portions

Ingredients
5 lbs pork shoulder (local suggestion: North Okanagan Game Meats)
2 1/4 cups Canadian whisky
2 1/4 cups maple syrup
1 1/2 cups brown sugar
7 oz coarse salt
7 oz sugar
3 bay leaves
4 cups apple juice (to cover pork shoulder) (local suggestion: Function Junction)
2 tbsp paprika
10 cloves garlic
2 bunches thyme
6 red chilies, fresh
2 jalapeño's, fresh
2 1/4 cups tomato paste
2 liters canned diced tomato
6 limes
2 white onions
2 bunches cilantro
8 oz pinto beans
4 Granny Smith apples
4 carrots
2 red onions
2 tbls honey
1 lb bacon
3/4 cup sour cream
1 per guest 6 " corn tortillas

Methods:
Brine:
Add coarse salt and sugar to cold water, bay leaves, 1 bunch thyme, half the maple syrup, and half the whiskey. Mix well until salt and sugar is dissolved. Clean excess fat off pork shoulder, cut into 1-2lb pieces, add to apple juice brine. Let sit in a refrigerator for 2 days.

Rub:
Towel dry pork after brine. In bowl mix paprika, 4 cloves garlic minced, fresh thyme leaves, black pepper, 1/2 cup olive oil, 1/4 cup brown sugar and let stand in refrigerator for 1 day.

Sear & Smoke:
In hot pan add olive oil and pork pieces, sear until browned on all sides. Remove from pan and place in a smoker, cold smoke for 4-6 hours.

BBQ Sauce:
In large sauce pot, add olive oil, diced white onions, 4 cloves garlic and jalapeños. Cook until onions start to caramel in color, add the remaining brown sugar, maple syrup, whiskey, 3 limes juice and zest.Add tomato paste, diced tomato with juice and half the chopped cilantro, cook for 20 minutes.

Braise:
In roasting pan place seared pork, add the BBQ sauce, (BBQ sauce should cover the top of the pork if not add tomato juice). Cover and place in oven at 300°F. Cook until meat is tender fall apart consistency approximately 4 hours. Remove BBQ sauce and in a separate pot reduce liquid to a thick BBQ sauce consistency. Cool. Shred pork, mix BBQ sauce and pork together, serve warm.

Pinto Beans:
Soak beans overnight in cold water, refrigerated. Next day, transfer beans and water to saucepan, add bacon, onion, garlic, 1 whole chili. Boil until beans are soft, strain off liquid, purée all together, cool and fold in sour cream.

Apple Lime Slaw:
Combine julienned/shredded Granny Smith tart apples, zest and juice of 3 limes, 4 medium carrots peeled & julienned / shredded, red onion julienned, red chilies julienned with chopped cilantro, olive oil and honey. Mix together, season with salt and pepper.

Assembly:
Fry corn tortilla in deep fryer, pushing it down with a metal ladle. Remove and cool at room temperature. Fill tortilla with warmed bean purée, pulled BBQ pork, apple slaw, serve and enjoy!

THE CHEF

Stuart Klassen, Executive Chef, Delta Grand Okanagan Resort & Conference Centre, Kelowna / President Okanagan Chefs Association

In his own words:
"Okanagan cuisine is the passion of local chefs using local farmers and purveyors found exclusively here in the Okanagan Valley. The Okanagan offers a vast variety of ingredients and of course, wines. The true Okanagan plate encompasses these philosophies from start to finish. Chefs use fresh fruits as they are harvested, but we also take the harvest and preserve it so our guests can enjoy the Okanagan flavours all year long. Besides fruit, we have amazing farmers that will produce any and all vegetables we request, we have local fish such as Okanagan Sockeye salmon, we have North Okanagan Game Meats providing chefs with pork, venison, lamb. Okanagan's Finest Angus Beef is used by our chefs

in the valley as well. Okanagan cuisine is chefs using what's in their backyard. The Inspiration to cook and serve my customers local food comes from all around me. The passion of our farmers and suppliers is amazing and they totally work with the chefs. The products are superior. My customers are usually traveling and want to taste what our region has to offer. It gives me and my team a great sense of pride in our sustainable practices.
My relationship with the farmers and artisans is very important as I create menus based on what they have and at what time of the year. Also If I need to plan a menu for the winter time I need to be sure I can have the produce in advance so I can preserve enough to last in the off season."

Stuart Klassen on the Okanagan Chefs Association:

"As the President of the Okanagan Chef Association CCFCC (Canadian Culinary Federation of Chefs and Cooks) in this region and Executive Chef of the Delta Grand Okanagan Resort & Conference Centre I have observed the unique chef culture here. We all work together like nowhere I have seen before. Our chefs host countless events and fundraisers to support our community. We work extremely closely with our farmers and local suppliers and together we have built a sustainable, creative and local culinary scene like no other in the country.

The Okanagan branch of the CCFCC has a strong focus on the junior chefs, from educational tours, working on fundraiser dinners and overall being part of the sustainable movement in the Okanagan Valley. This team of junior chefs play an active role in such events as Feast of Fields, Farm 2 Chef, Canadian National CCFCC Junior Exchange, to name a few.

I am proud of our community and support its growth any way I can to ensure the culinary chefs in wine country continue to work together in harmony with the each other and our local farmers and suppliers."

The Farmers/Cidermakers

Glenn & Loretta Cross, Function Junction/Double Cross Cidery, Kelowna

Farming blood runs deep in Glenn Cross' family on both sides. Glenn's Grandfather George Whelan (on his mother's side) was actually the first commercial grower in the Okanagan Valley in 1884! He owned 3298 acres, mostly rangeland, but also had orchards and made apple cider. In 1944 Glenn's parents, Elwyn and Joy Cross bought the 50-acre orchard where Function Junction now operates .

Glenn has been on the BC Fruit Packers Co-Op Board of Directors and was President of BC Tree Fruits - he currently sits on the Grower's Supply Board of Directors. Glenn was instrumental in the amalgamation of the four Packing Houses in the Okanagan Valley.

Loretta Cross runs the Function Junction Fruit Stand on the farm. "It was always my dream to own and operate a fruit stand. We have recognized the importance of diversification over the years, so we have planted blackberries, raspberries, red currants, grapes and then moved into a wide variety of soft fruit such as plums, peaches and apricots. We then expanded to include a wide variety of vegetables including nine acres of corn, and are also leasing a blueberry patch."

Last year they acquired Kelowna Land and Orchard's juice and cider equipment. "Nicole Bullock worked with us to get us up and running so now we are making our very own 100% pure Function Junction apple juice. We use a UV machine to pasteurize our juice, ensuring no heating of the product, so all the nutrients stay in the juice! "

PAIRING

Double Cross Apple Cider

In 2012 the Crosses were licensed to open on-site Double Cross Cidery. They now produce their own line of Iced Cider as well as a Hard Apple Cider. The Iced Ciders are a concentrated elixir that is hand crafted by freezing fresh pressed apple or pear juice and then slowly fermented.

SOCKEYE SALMON, ZUCCHINI FRITTERS w/ROMESCO SAUCE

CHEF: JEFF VAN GEEST, MIRADORO RESTAURANT, OLIVER
FARMER: GORDON FORBES, FORBES FARMS, OLIVER
WINEMAKER: FAIRVIEW CELLARS, OLIVER

Zucchini fritters are an underrated delicacy. Easy to make, and so delicious when made in season, they can be served casually or at a formal table. Jeff uses mint in this recipe but you can substitute other herbs like basil or lemon thyme. Using local Sockeye salmon has been an exciting addition to Okanagan cuisine.

Serves 6

Romesco Sauce:
1/4 cup almonds, blanched
1/4 cup hazelnuts, peeled
1 head of garlic
1 slice of stale white bread (good quality is best)
2 medium sized ripe tomatoes
2 large red peppers, roasted, peeled and seeded
1 cup extra virgin olive oil
1/2 cup sherry vinegar
1/4 tsp chili flakes

Purée all ingredients in a food processor. Season as needed

Zucchini Fritters:
2 – 4 zucchinis (about 2 lbs)
3 tbsp salt
1 cup all purpose flour
1 lemon, zest and juice
2 tbsp chives, chopped
2 tbsp mint, chopped
2 eggs - beaten

Grate zucchini, add salt and mix. Place in a colander in a sink and let the zucchini sit for about 20 minutes to drain. Squeeze out excess moisture then mix in remaining ingredients. Pour a tablespoon or so of olive oil into a non-stick pan that has been heated to medium. Spoon about a half cup of mix into the pan and flatten into a pancake about 1 cm thick. Fry until both sides are golden and crisp and the interior is cooked - about 5 minutes. Repeat until all the mix is made into pancakes and reserve.

Salmon:
6 - 5 ounce portions of (preferably) fresh local Sockeye salmon, scaled, with skin on
sea salt and fresh cracked black pepper
olive oil

Preheat your oven to 425°F.
Heat a non-stick sauté pan on the stove to medium high heat. Season the skin side of the salmon lightly. Place the salmon into the pans and cook on the stovetop until the skin starts to crisp and get golden. Finish in the oven until the flesh is just medium rare in the middle.

Assembly:
Spread a dollop of Romesco sauce on 6 plates. Place a zucchini fritter on each plate and the salmon on top of that, skin side up to show off that beautiful crispy skin!
Serve with a platter of roasted summer vegetables drizzled in good quality olive oil.

97

(L-R) Bill Eggert.
Gordon Forbes and
Chef Jeff Van Geest.

THE CHEF

Jeff Van Geest, Executive Chef, Miradoro Restaurant, Oliver

Born and raised in St. Catharines, Ontario, Jeff Van Geest hit the Vancouver culinary scene as apprentice then Sous Chef at the iconic Bishop's Restaurant - pioneers in sustainable, seasonal farm to table cuisine. He went on to open his own raved about restaurant Aurora Bistro winning several prestigious awards. Growing up with farmers as grandparents, Jeff developed his respect for fresh local produce at a very early age.

In his own words:
"I was drawn to the Okanagan by the natural beauty, the wine, the proximity to the farmers, the escape from the city and the house prices.

My favourite ingredient is whatever is seasonal and coming in the back door of the kitchen, however, if I had to choose one, I would say peaches. I have a very strong childhood memory of eating warm, ripe peaches right off the tree in Southern Ontario. Eating good peaches now always brings me back to those times (like that scene in Ratatouille). (I am) excited to be able to essentially be working 'next door' to the farmers that supply me the local ingredients on the menu.
I see a slow and steady growth for the culinary industry here in the Okanagan. I would love to see more high quality casual places opening. We have lots of great high end dining options, but more cheap and casual places that do it right would be great."

THE FARMER

Forbes Farm, Gordon Forbes, Oliver

Forbes Farm is a 12.9-acre home farm of fruit, vegetables, and free-range animals located just north of Oliver. The Forbes family has operated the farm since 1974 (organically since 1995) and are members of LEOGA (Living Earth Organic Growers Association) and Certified Naturally Grown. They are also were one of the first farms in Canada to be certified salmon safe and the first farm in the Okanagan to be made a conservation partner with The Land Conservancy of BC.

In his own words:

"Organic farming is a very honorable pursuit, working in harmony with nature and all the creative forces of the living world. We enjoy sharing good, healthy food with local families. I would like to see every community take the example of Nelson Kootenay Co-op. This is the hub of the community, bringing food, health and healing together. Farmers markets are also an important part, as

they bring consumers and farmers together to talk about the local food that is being grown and eaten. More people these days want to know where their food is coming from and who is producing it.

For the culinary future of the area, I would like to see more education on how to prepare and preserve the local bounty. These are lost arts and people need to be re-educated about their importance. We may spend more to buy local organic produce but we save money by preparing the food ourselves.

All the farm animals at our farm perform various vital functions in the growth of fruit and vegetables. Our free-range chickens happily scratch around the trees and our turkeys contribute (either with grazing or as natural composters of all the vegetative material). Our pigs help turn over the ground to prepare for the coming crop and happily consume any culled fruit and vegetables."

THE WINEMAKER

Fairview Cellars, Oliver

Known as the "Cab Man", Bill Eggert has been creating high quality Cabernet based wines at his winery up in the hills of Oliver. On his 6-acre vineyard, Bill grows premium Cabernet Sauvignon on half the land and Merlot and Cabernet Franc on the other. A row of Syrah and Petit Verdot are on site with some Sauvignon Blanc – his only white wine.

Many of the names of his wines have a very interesting story attached. Two Hoots is named for the two little owls that patrol his vineyard.

Bill's 2009 The Wrath is a heavenly creation and its epic name is appropriate. Not only because of its divine depth and rich palette of flavours, but also because some godly force helped create the bizarre weather conditions that contributed to its making. Battered brutally by the wrath of Mother Nature,

hail virtually destroyed one side of his Cabernet Sauvignon vines. His first thought was to let the grapes hang and ignore the mess, the second was "what the hell" and he salvaged the clusters which had some skins and pulp still in tact as well as untouched bunches that had been protected from the wind blown hail. He pressed. He waited. He tasted. The result was a concentrated, rich wine – similar to Italy's famous Amarone wines made from semi-dried grapes. Will he be able to make it again? We can only hope.

Bill can be found around the vineyard (he is grower and winemaker here) or in the rustic cabin on the estate that acts as his tasting room. Inside you may find him banging on the keyboard of his piano or teaching his new dog DJ (short for Duke Jr.) some old tricks.

PAIRING

2009 Fairview Cellars MadCap Red

This wine was named for Bill himself (known by many as the madcap winemaker), and is a blend of Merlot, Cabernet Sauvignon and Cabernet Franc – heavy on the Merlot. Rich blackberries, cocoa and spice roll around your palate in a velvet coat.

WILD BC SPOT PRAWN RISOTTO W/ GREEN CITY ACRES ORGANIC GREENS

CHEF BERNARD CASAVANT, MANTEO RESORT, KELOWNA
FARMER: CURTIS STONE, GREEN CITY ACRES, KELOWNA
WINEMAKER: SANDHILL ESTATE WINERY, KELOWNA

The creamy Okanagan goat cheese in this recipe works beautifully with the prawns. The Viognier's aromatics transform this combination into a celebration dish. Make sure to use high quality Arborio or Carnaroli rice from Italy.
Author's note: I order the Cascina Veneria Carnaroli Rice as well as all of my olive oil from Italy through local Kelowna girl, Teresa Kuhn's import company, The Olive Oil Merchant. Teresa went over to Italy for a holiday and ended up marrying a local. This company was born of that relationship and they now run it from Kelowna. www.oliveoilmerchant.com

Ingredients:
1 litre vegetable stock
1 tbsp butter
1 tbsp olive oil
1 cup onion, peeled, diced fine
1 cup Arborio rice
1/2 cup B.C. white wine
30 Wild BC Spot Prawns, peeled (reserve shells for another use) * depending on the size of the prawns, and how much you like them!
1 tbsp butter
1 1/2 cups fresh Okanagan chevre (goats cheese) (local suggestion: Carmelis Goat Cheese)
sea salt, milled pepper to taste
2 tbsp chives, finely minced

Method:
Bring stock to a rolling boil, reduce to a simmer.
In a pot large enough to hold all ingredients, over medium heat, heat the oil and butter, add the onion. Sauté briefly until soft. Do not allow it to brown. Add the Arborio, sauté until well coated, and the Arborio changes to a light white color. Add in the white wine, stir and reduce.
Using a 4 oz ladle, carefully add the stock one ladle at a time, stirring until the liquid is almost evaporated. Repeat procedure, adding the stock until the stock is almost finished.
When the rice is fully cooked, and still a little crunchy in the center (al dente) stop adding stock, fold in the Spot Prawns, and mix thoroughly. Do not over mix as the Risotto will become mushy. Add in the butter, chevre, salt, milled pepper. Mix again, taste, adjust the seasoning if necessary.
Add in a half ladle of stock and chives, mix very lightly. Serve immediately and enjoy!

SPOT PRAWNS are the largest of the 7 commercial species of shrimp found on the West Coast of Canada. Although not technically an Okanagan ingredient, 2012 marked the The 2nd Annual Okanagan Spot Prawn Festival in Kelowna. Chef Robert Clark from Vancouver's C Restaurant was responsible "basically for reintroducing spot prawns to the BC culinary scene". Jon Crofts, owner of Kelowna's Codfathers Seafood Market, who also spearheaded the Okanagan Festival here, says "previously, 90% of prawns were being exported to Asia, so Rob got together with some progressive local fishermen and decided to change this. With the help of the Chefs Table Society, they started the Vancouver Spot Prawn Festival to increase public awareness of the product, and to stimulate local demand in order to get the fishermen the price locally that they could get abroad for the prawns. It became a great success, and has spawned other festivals in the province including our own, so that now our Prawns are 80% consumed in Canada."
www.wildbcspotprawns.com

THE CHEF

Bernard Casavant, Manteo Resort

Born and trained in British Columbia, Chef Bernard's cooking career began with the encouragement of his grandmother and was further nurtured by a career guidance counselor in Grade 9. Torn between a career as a soccer player or a Chef, Chef Bernard chose the career that would ensure he would never be hungry. His grandmother instilled a strong work ethic in the young chef, along with "the passion for respecting the food and the people who produce it."

Chef Bernard received his certified Chef de Cuisine certification in 1986, one of the inaugural chefs in Canada to complete the exam. He is a member at large of the BC Restaurant and Food Association, and sits as Director of BC Culinary Tourism Society. Chef Bernard is a member of the Okanagan Chefs Association, the Canadian Culinary Association and is a BC Restaurant Hall of Fame Inductee. Also a talented artist, Chef Bernard creates beautiful wood serving platters and has been known to draw his dishes first to instruct his staff on his vision. In earlier years, those drawings were framed and hung on the walls at his Whistler restaurant.

In this own words:

"Growing up on Vancouver Island, our family always vacationed in the Okanagan Valley, enjoying the fantastic fruits and lakes. After spending 18 years in Whistler, my wife Bonnie and I decided to re-locate to the Okanagan as we both enjoy the climate and the easy accessibility of top quality artisan foods and wines. My favorite local ingredient is definitely Harker's heirloom tomatoes. The diversity of color, flavor and textures is absolutely amazing. As a chef, it is so easy to impress our guests with one of our tomato tasting platters. We also preserve a massive amount of tomatoes, to be enjoyed by our guests in the restaurant and the ballroom during the winter months.

Another attraction for myself is the vibrant culinary scene in the valley. This is due to the fact that a lot of top level chefs have moved to the valley in recent years, and they are requesting top quality ingredients from our producers. Supporting the farmers is both fundamental and key to long term growth of our tourism sector.

If I were to draw out and color my vision for the future, it would include a totally integrated teaching academy, blending the various arts on one campus. Included would be the farmers, wine makers, cheese producers, artisan salumieres, wood craftsman and the various artist mediums. Couple this with further education studies for the hospitality industry and it would be great. It is all about the youth, and keeping them in the industry. I understand that we did have a tomato processing plant in the Lillooet area in the 50's, I think it is only a matter of time before we have a major processing plant here in the Okanagan. Being able to produce top quality boutique items for the world market would definitely give our economy a boost year round, and give a reason for farmers to harvest their products."

(L-R) Chef Bernard Casavant, Curtis Stone and Howard Soon

THE FARMER

Curtis Stone, Green City Acres, Kelowna

Located in downtown Kelowna, Green City Acres is a 3/4-acre urban farm, operating on eight plots throughout the city. Without enough land or capital to start his own growing operation, Curtis utilized innovative strategy provided to him by the SPIN program in the US where they "rent" garden space from homeowners. All produce is grown with natural methods, meaning that no chemical fertilizers, sprays, or pesticides are used.

To take their green lifestyle a step further, Green City Acres is pedal-powered, meaning that all of their business – deliveries etc. – are done on bicycles and custom-built trailers. Fresh produce deliveries to restaurants and the farmers' market and transporting their compost and equipment is all done on wheels.

Their veggie box delivery service, or CSA (Community Supported Agriculture) Curtis says, "is a way of directly connecting the eaters to the growers and removing the middle man and taking the exchange out of the common commerce." Good news is he says recently, "I'm noticing a lot more younger people shopping at the farmers market now too."

In his own words:
"I was born and raised here, but left when I was 20. I came back because I felt terrified with where society was heading, and I wanted to be close to my family. I felt Kelowna was a great place to start my business because there was nothing like this here and people were starving for something unique that was part of the solution to a lot of the problems we face.

SPIN Farming showed me that it was possible to make a living from farming land you don't own, and with very little investment. It seemed like my only option. All I wanted to do was live by my values, and homesteading in a traditional sense, was the only way I could do that. But how does a guy who doesn't want to sign his life away to the bank for 30 years, get a piece of property to farm on? SPIN was the answer to that for me. Firstly, I can grow all the fresh produce I need for myself and my family, thereby removing myself as best I can from the conventional system. And, I can actually make a good living at it. I was sold.

I would like to see young people who are disenfranchised with the 'system' to start a career in farming. I believe that if we want to change the system, protesting in the street does nothing. We need to recreate the system ourselves. First, we need to start with localized food production, then that can move into localized economies of scale and trade. I think the future of SPIN farming here can be great, because we have an amazing growing climate, and we have thousands of huge lawns all over this city, just waiting to be turned up."

THE WINEMAKER

Howard Soon, Sandhill Winery, Kelowna

Legendary local Winemaker Howard Soon describes his winemaking technique "gentle" and "non-interventionist." Born and raised in Vancouver, Howard is one of the true pioneers in the BC wine industry and has been the Head Winemaker at Sandhill since 1997. His wines are made from six unique Okanagan vineyards resulting in an array of single vineyard wines that reflect the terroir of each property. The Small Lots program takes the art of winemaking to another level with Howard paying extra attention to distinctive barrels from each vintage.

PAIRING

Sandhill 2011 Small Lots Viognier

An aromatic beauty, this special Viognier displays a bouquet of exotic fruits, perfumed flowers and ripe local pears to your nose. Fat and rich with flavours, this is wine to savour.

DESSERTS

AN OKANAGAN
CHEESE BOARD

APPLE TARTE TATIN

CHEF: SANDRINE MARTIN-RAFFAULT, OWNER/CHEF SANDRINE FRENCH PASTRY &
CHOCOLATE, KELOWNA
FARMER: BOB CALLIOUX, KELOWNA FARMERS' & CRAFTERS MARKET
WINEMAKER: BELLA WINES, SUMMERLAND

This delicious French tarte is basically an upside down pie. Impressive to serve with the dramatic flip and all – this dish tastes difficult but is quite easy to make. Chef Sandrine is known for her world-class desserts and chocolates. Through this dish, she shares a little bit of her French magic using beautiful Okanagan apples.

Method

For the caramel:
300 g sugar
100g water

Put sugar and water in a pot. Wait until the sugar is "dissolved" in the water (all the sugar needs to be wet). Place the pot on the stove (highest temperature) and cook until the sugar gets a nice blond caramel colour. Pour immediately into the pie dish.
Peel and cut apples into quarter pieces (6 to 12 apples according the size of the pie dish).
Place the apple pieces nicely in the pie dish. Add about 50 g of butter cut in small pieces.
Place the dough (see recipe paté brisée) over the apples and fold around the edge.
Cook for about 45 min to an hour at 350 °F.
Cool for 10 to 20 min. Flip the tart on a plate.
Serve warm with vanilla ice cream, crème Anglaise or Chantilly.

Pate Brisee

250 g flour (2 cups)
125 g butter
1 egg yolk
a pinch of sugar
a pinch of salt
tarte size: 8 to 10 inches

Mix with the paddle attachment all of the ingredients. When you press the dough in your hand and it stays "compact", remove the dough from the bowl mixer and knead with your hands until it forms a nice and smooth ball. Add a little bit of water if necessary.
Flatten the ball of dough. Wrap it tightly and store in the refrigerator for at least an hour.
Spread a thin layer of flour on the counter and roll the dough until it is about 2 millimeters thick.

THE CHEF

Sandrine Martin-Raffault, Sandrine French Pastry & Chocolate, Kelowna

Sandrine Martin-Raffault grew up in the Beaujolais region of France and was trained as a pastry chef. In 2004, Sandrine, her husband Pierre-Jean and their two children moved to Kelowna where they opened La Boulangerie in the Mission. Two years ago, Sandrine French Pastry & Chocolate, an artisan chocolate and fine dessert patisserie, was born.

In her own words:
"French cuisine has a long history, which comes with it pros and cons. French are sometimes a prisoner of their culture, their history, and their tradition hence not as creative as cooks from the Okanagan. They rely so much on their cuisine that they don't explore, steal and adapt techniques or ideas from other countries. This is the creativity of the cooks with an inspirational international twist that I enjoy the most in the Okanagan. As a mother, I was extremely surprised about multiple things when we arrived in BC. From

an early age, children are taught differently about food. In France, children have a two hour break for lunch, where they either go back home for lunch break or stay at school and eat at the cantine (cafeteria supplying a full meal with appetizer, entrée, cheese or yogurt and dessert). Therefore children are used to eating a full meal every day, hot, seated at a table, with forks and knife, drinking water (usually no pop allowed). A child eating a cold tuna sandwich in 20 minutes with a few carrots on the side and a pop for lunch is inconceivable in most French families. I am not saying this is better or worse, I am just stating how it is a main factor, which changes a person's relationship with food from an early age.
The change I would hope to see for our future? A simplified relationship with food. Not the French way, which cannot for many reasons be transferred here, but in a new Canadian way still to be defined."

THE FARMER

Kelowna Farmers' Market, Bob Callioux

Like many local chefs, Sandrine sources her apples and other produce from our Kelowna farmers market. Open year round, the market has grown exponentially over the years and has an exciting future ahead. Market Manager Bob Cailloux has been involved with the Market since the early days and has grown with it over the years.

In his own words:
"I was raised on a farm in Wildwood, Alberta. I studied commercial cooking at the Northern Alberta Institute of Technology before establishing a catering business in Edmonton for 15 years.
We came to the Okanagan in 1992 for a change in lifestyle. A year later I was making willow furniture and joined a small farmers' market in downtown Kelowna.

When the farmers' market was asked to leave their site I spearheaded the formation of the present Kelowna Farmers' Market with help from Orchard Park Mall with a loan of $350.00 for a license to operate.
We started out with four vendors and today we have over 165 vendors gather on Wednesday and Saturday mornings. With education on buying local food and supporting our farmers, more and more people including young families are shopping at the farmers' market . Today we have over 5000 customers on a Wednesday and Saturday morning shopping for fresh local products. My hope for the future is that within five years we will see the Kelowna Farmers' Market moving to a new permanent home, where the community can be proud of one of the best farmers' markets in Canada."

THE WINEMAKER

Bella Wines, Summerland

Jay Drysdale has been a part of the Okanagan wine scene for many years. Now a Winemaker, Jay has his own label, Bella Wines named for his beloved bulldog, Bella whom he shared with wife, Wendy. Being a winemaker is a dream come true.

In his own words:
"Bella's Story – let's see. I call it a wine geek's love story. From the moment I finished my ISG (International Sommelier Guild) diploma, I foresaw that BC had what it takes to become a world-class wine region. I have spent the last 8-9 years as a part of the industry and it's been incredible to experience its growth. I have worked every aspect of this industry and when I caught the winemaking bug about 4 years ago, I knew making wine was in my future. Then I met the love of my life and my dream became our dream and now a reality.

The industry has taught me that I needed to balance look and quality. The wine needs to be sexy and appealing to any consumer, but still have a serious side that will earn its respect over time. Our first vintage is exciting as it all comes to fruition, but I even more excited knowing exactly what I want it to be 10 years from now.
I'm honoured to have Michael Bartier in my corner at Okanagan Crush Pad and I know that Bella's efforts coupled with the amazing products from other wineries, will over time, increase our worldly respect one vintage at a time.
Okanagan cuisine is transforming at an even faster rate as chefs are connecting with the farmers and shaping the landscape together. We see more and more interest into heirloom varieties while not losing respect for our natural ingredients. We are seeing a genuine desire to grow the healthiest produce possible and organic is almost the baseline, as farmers are really seeking balance. "

PAIRING

Rest in Peace Bella

Bella Sparkling Wine, Gamay Rosé

This beautiful, blush hued wine literally winks at you with its sexy white label and pretty design. The bubbles happily hop onto your palate with a burst of freshness. Elegant and crisp with rhubarb and strawberry notes, this wine pairs well with ladies who lunch and picnics at the beach.

BLUEBERRY & ALMOND FINANCIER WITH UPPER BENCH BRIE

CHEF: GIULIO PICCOLI, THE ROTTEN GRAPE, KELOWNA
CHEESEMAKER: SHANA MILLER, UPPER BENCH CHEESE, PENTICTON
WINEMAKER: UPPER BENCH WINERY, PENTICTON

A financier is a French pastry usually containing almonds and beurre noisette (brown butter). Rita Myers, owner of The Rotten Grape and Giulio are very conscious of offering delicious menu choices for those with food allergies and buckwheat flour makes this a gluten-free recipe. Giulio also points out that this is a great way to use up egg whites left over from other recipes!

Ingredients:

Upper Bench Brie - as much as you wish
75 g butter, unsalted
1 cup icing sugar
1 tsp baking powder
5 tbsp buckwheat flour
3 egg whites
1/2 cup blueberries plus more for decoration*
75 gr. almonds, ground
splash of amaretto
* frozen blueberries work well too.

Take the Brie out of the fridge and allow for its temperature to raise slowly. This is important for most foods, and especially for cheese, to be enjoyed at its true best - a sort of decanting.
Preheat the oven at 375ºF.
Melt the butter on low heat. The solids will separate and sink to the bottom while they start browning, giving the characteristic toasty hazelnut color typical of brown butter. Allow to cool and strain through a cheesecloth.
Roast the ground almonds for a few minutes, until they start to change color to a light golden brown.
In a bowl or in a mixer with the paddle attachment, mix your dry ingredients: icing sugar, ground almonds and flour.

Add the egg whites, one at the time, making sure that the first one is well incorporated before adding the second one. Now add your butter: The mixture should be sticky. Add blueberries, making sure to add all of the juices that might be left in the bowl; they will give a much lovelier color to the mix. Add a splash of amaretto. ("I think that it would be wonderful to serve the dessert with a blueberry tea... and even more perfect for a cold winter night by the fire." - Giulio). Pour into regular muffin/cupcake tin; fill it almost to the top. Bake for 15-17 minutes at 375ºF . Use the toothpick test to check if it is done (insert a toothpick –if it comes out clean your dish is ready.) It should be slightly crisp and golden brown around the edges. Allow to cool for 10 minutes.

To serve:
Guilio suggests making a little berry sauce to decorate the plate with, nothing more than a few blueberries reduced in their own juices for a few minutes.
Drizzle some of the sauce on a plate, place your Brie cut in a neat wedge with your financier close by, opla'!

THE CHEF

Giulio Piccoli, The Rotten Grape, Kelowna

Giulio is the Chef at The Rotten Grape Wine & Espresso Bar in downtown Kelowna. He brought with him the flavours of Italy, enhancing their menu with the tastes of his hometown. Follow his cooking adventures and discoveries on Facebook: /foodistherevolution/

In his own words:
"Born and raised in a small town in Emilia Romagna, I decided to, well, run away from home at 19.
I met a beautiful Canadian woman who made me curious about a country I knew nothing about and I decided to follow her to an even smaller town in northern Ontario, Kapuskasing. After a few months there, I realized how much I missed my mother's cooking and decided I was going to learn how to cook like her. I immediately fell in love with the feeling of being in a kitchen, playing with knives, fire and new ingredients, and so I started to cook with some amazing chefs both in Canada and Italy. In 2008 I worked for a year in an incredible restaurant in Forte dei

Marmi, Toscana. This experience really changed the way I approach food, and it was also my first encounter with the slow food philosophy, which is now the driving force in what I do.

The warm Okanagan summer, with its beautiful products, did the rest to convince me to move here.
What I really love about the valley is that as I spent more time here, I realized how this area of the world is really developing its unique culinary identity: It is not trying to copy anybody but is carried through by the knowledge and passion of the artisan behind it. I find this very unique to Canada and at the same time very familiar with where I came from, and this is why it very much feels like home here.
I would love for chefs to become less culinary artists and more culinary teachers, filling in the gaps, and raising awareness in people on how important food is, not just to satisfy our palates or for our health, but for the community as a whole."

THE WINE & CHEESEMAKER

Gavin and Shana Miller, Upper Bench Wine & Cheese, Penticton

It was a combination of passions that brought owners Gavin and Shana Miller together many years ago. He, a winemaker from the UK, she a cheesemaker from Nova Scotia, now married 16 years, their dream of opening their own business was realized this year.

In her own words:
Ramblings from the (self-named) "Curd Nurd" Shana Miller: "The Okanagan is like playground for foodies - glorious, bountiful, and there's continuously something new to eat, sip and experience. As consumers become more food educated, we are asking more questions - how was it made, where did it come from, who put their love into it and why? We now seek not only quality, but the experience too - the story. We want to know the 'why, where and how' from producers, who are more than happy to share their story. Everyone has a story to share and people enjoy knowing what they are eating was loved, whether it be animal, vegetable, fruit (or cheese!). I believe this way of appreciating food will ensure that the generations to come will be more healthy, happy and appreciative of our planet and all its offerings.
I remember the first time I made cheese commercially, the smell of the warming milk was reminiscent of cold Nova Scotia winters being made just a little easier with a mug of warmed milk. After the milk has been warmed, cultures added, renneted - just a short time later, when it is time to remove the lids, I still marvel at the transformation of a liquid to a solid sweet smelling mass of curd. Just amazing. I feel so blessed to have found my craft and even more so to have the ability to share with others and to have the support, making what I do a dream come true - it is truly humbling."

In his own words:
"What makes Naramata Bench so special? Almost virgin soil, clean air and an amazing intensity of light all help to produce some of the most unaffected wines in the world. Here we can grow fresh, clean wines with great intensity and purity of fruit.

We live on the edge, never quite knowing if we will ripen our harvest before the first frost, always begging Mother Nature for a few more degrees of heat or days of sunshine.
Miraculously every year seems to bring better product, a better understanding of the terroir with which we work, better vineyard practices, and slowly new levels of recognition from our local and international peers. It is such a joy to be part of such a young, yet blossoming industry, where competitors share knowledge and recommend each other for the common good.
To me, wine is made in a vineyard. The attention to detail, the love, if you like, that each vine receives during the growing season reflects in every sip. I once had the fortune to chat to the Estate Director for Chateau Margaux, and being a winemaker I asked. 'Who makes the wine?' his answer was 'Nobody. Wine makes itself- we are here just to guide it through the process. To keep it on track, to nudge it in the right direction, to put our own stamp on it's creation.' Years later I couldn't agree more."

CHOCOLATE CUPCAKES w/ NARAMATA RASPBERRY SAUCE

CHEF: STEWART GLYNES, THE BENCH ARTISAN FOOD MARKET, PENTICTON
HOME FARMER: JULIA GRIFFITH, NARAMATA
WINEMAKER: ELEPHANT ISLAND ESTATE WINERY, NARAMATA

Who doesn't love chocolate cupcakes? This delicious version becomes extra special with the addition of local raspberries and Elephant Island fruit wine.

Cupcakes:
10 eggs
500 g sugar
680 g good quality dark chocolate
340 g unsalted butter
120 g cocoa powder

Melt chocolate and butter over a water bath. Whisk eggs and sugar in mixer on high until pale and fluffy. Add melted chocolate and butter mixture slowly to incorporate. Whisk on high for 2 minutes. Add cocoa powder slowly to incorporate. Divide evenly amongst 24 lined muffin tins. Bake at 325ºF for 40-45 minutes.

Raspberry Puree:
400 g fresh Naramata raspberries*
3 tbsp Okanagan honey (local suggestion: Arlo's Honey, Kelowna)
2 tsp lemon juice
1/4 cup Elephant Island Framboise
Frozen raspberries can be substituted.

Blend raspberries, honey and Frambroise in food processor. Strain to remove seeds.

To serve, place one cupcake on a plate and drizzle with Raspberry Purée.

THE CHEF

Stewart Glynes,
The Bench Artisan Food Market,
Penticton

The Bench Artisan Food Market was born from a lifelong passion for good food and sharing good food with others. In July 2005, sisters Dawn Lennie and Debbie Halladay purchased an old corner store in Penticton that was on the way to the growing Naramata Bench wine route. The store was renovated and reopened as The Bench Artisan Food Market in September 2005 with the mantra of serving top quality food and drink and offering artisanal grocery in a fun, friendly atmosphere.

In Dawn's own words:
"The recipe supplied here is from Chef Stewart Glynes, 'the guy' at The Bench who makes it all happen in the kitchen. The pairing with Elephant Island Pink Elephant is a family affair with owners Del and Miranda Halladay - Del is Dawn's and Deb's brother. The raspberries used in this recipe were sourced from Miranda's Mom Julia who lovingly grows them in her amazing backyard vegetable garden in Naramata. Her vegetables feed on luscious dirt hand crafted by Miranda's father, Rhys, who composts all of the organic waste from The Bench Market year round!
That's one of the things that is so great about living in the Okanagan, the abundance of fresh fruits and vegetables and the passion and creativity of the people who grow, cook or create wonderful and tasty food in the Okanagan.
I hope that the future of food is fresh, healthy and local! I hope that parents and schools start to teach kids where their food comes from, the awesome nutritional value of good food and how to cook it and become excited about it themselves. I hope we become less 'big box' and more 'mom and pop' – this is much better for the proprietor, the consumer and the community. I think we are already on our way in the sunny Okanagan!"

Dawn Lennie (L) with Stewart Glynes

THE FARMER

Julia Griffith, Naramata

Julia Griffith provides the raspberries for the recipe as well as grows a wide array of other vegetables, herbs and berries for The Bench Market, the Penticton and Summerland Farmers Markets and other businesses in Naramata. The Bench Market and Elephant Island Winery are a great example of a family effort - with everyone contributing their talents.

In her own words:
"I am from Powell River (originally). I taught there for over 30 years. My mom and dad lived in Naramata - it was their retirement property/dream. My daughter, Miranda and her husband came to Naramata 13 years ago and with my mom's encouragement began the Elephant Island Winery. When I

retired from teaching we moved to Naramata where we have a large garden. My husband is interested in composting and has built a good composting system, using the vegetable/kitchen waste from The Bench Market. He's managed to build up the soil, which previously had been almost impenetrable clay - thus the productive garden.
I've been growing veggies for over 30 years. It's a joy to grow veggies in the Okanagan, after the challenges of gardening on the Coast (slugs, blights). What astounds me is the amount of food that can be produced on a relatively small plot with good soil and the amazing Okanagan sun!"

THE WINEMAKER

Elephant Island Winery, Naramata

Miranda and Del Halladay founded the winery in 1999 in partnership with Miranda's Grandmother, Catherine Chard Wisnicki. Miranda's Grandfather, Paul, experimented with fruit winemaking and distilling and left behind his recipes brought from the old world, which are the foundation for all of the wines at Elephant Island.

Winemaker Christine Leroux trained at L'Institut D'Oenologie de Bordeaux, in Bordeaux, France combined with work experience at Chateau Petrus, Chateau Margaux and Cassegrain.
The name? "Grandmother Catherine acquired the orchard as a retirement investment. Grandfather Paul, or Poppy as we called him, was convinced that the investment would prove a "white elephant."

In 1972 Grandma Catherine's free spirit won... she purchased the property in Naramata and convinced Poppy this was "the" location for their dream home. Grandma is an architect (one of the first women in Canada) and Poppy an engineer. Collectively they proceeded to battle their respective opinions and collaborated on their coup de grace, the house at Elephant Island. Out of this clash of professional wills (Grandma's visual versus Grandfather's logical) emerged Poppy's name for the property... the architects "EYE-land" - testament to his perception of Grandma's obsession with the aesthetic.
WHITE ELEPHANT + Grandma's "EYE"LAND
Elephant Island... Grandma's way of getting back at Poppy for all of his mockery."

PAIRING

2010 Pink Elephant Sparkling Fruit Wine

Pink, flirty and fun! This wine becomes an instant favorite for those lucky enough to quaff. A Granny Smith apple cuvee with a cassis dosage makes for a bubbling party on your tongue.

Loukoumades (Greek Donuts) in Honey w/ Roasted Red Haven Peaches, Honey Sabayon & Lemon Verbena Ice Cream

Chef: Wayne Morris, Waterfront Restaurant & Wine Bar, Kelowna
Farmer: Helen Kennedy, Arlo's Honey, Kelowna
Winemaker: La Frenz Winery, Naramata

Peaches and honey – are you kidding me? The two sweet and delicious Okanagan delicacies in this dish are a combination from heaven. This recipe is a tribute to the honeybee and their dedicated beekeepers, like Helen Kennedy, who are passionate about educating people on the crucial roll of these buzzing honeymakers in our earth's future. Love a bee today.

Ice cream:
3 cups or 750g whipping cream
1 vanilla bean
5 g lemon verbena leaves
8 egg yolks
150 g Arlo's honey

Bring cream to a boil add lemon verbena and allow to steep, stirring occasionally for 20 minutes. Whisk together egg yolks, sugar and scraped vanilla bean pods. Bring cream to a boil and strain. Temper hot cream into the sugar egg yolk mixture. Cook mixture until it reaches 170ºF; strain and cool. Spin in an ice cream machine until frozen.

Honey Syrup:
500 g sugar
250 ml water
300 g Arlos honey
4 drops rosewater (local suggestion: Okanagan Lavender Farm)
1 stick cinnamon
4 cloves

Bring syrup to a boil for five minutes remove from heat and reserve.

Loukoumades:
500 g flour
500 g water
5 g instant yeast
5 g honey
2 g salt

Mix together all ingredients thoroughly and let stand at room temperature for two hours. Preheat deep fryer to 375ºF. Fry until golden (about 5 minutes) then immediately toss in syrup.

Roasted Red Haven Peaches:
Halve peaches and remove stones. Place in an oven at 300ºF for 10 minutes until they are just becoming tender. Peel.

Sabayon:
4 egg yolks
150 g Arlo's honey
100ml Okanagan white wine
50ml lemon juice

Over double boiler whisk sugar, wine, eggs until sauce reaches ribbon consistency.

THE CHEF

Wayne Morris, Restaurant Chef, Waterfront Restaurant & Wine Bar, Kelowna

Born in Yarmouth County, Nova Scotia, Wayne was taught to hunt, fish and raise animals from an early age. He attended Akerley NSCC from 2004-2006 studying Culinary Arts and then went on to work in a fine dining restaurant by the name of Stories in a boutique hotel in Halifax under the guidance of Chef Scott Vail. Wayne was first introduced to the Okanagan by his sommelier while studying wine in Culinary School. In 2007 he met Chef Mark Filatow in what was then "a quaint little wine bar in Kelowna." Serendipity intervened and two weeks later he started working at Waterfront Restaurant & Wine Bar.

In his own words:
"Two things inspire me to cook locally: the quality of the ingredients and the producers that make it possible. When I think my job is challenging I think about farming. The faith farmers have and the amount of work required to produce food and wine takes a special kind of person.

Relationships with suppliers are paramount, particularly in a small restaurant like Waterfront. We make virtually everything in house and want to offer the best dining experience possible. Without quality ingredients all of our efforts would be wasted. Sometimes we find the suppliers ourselves at the farmers' markets or while traveling locally. Sometimes we hear about a supplier from another chef or farmer. Occasionally they show up at the restaurant's front door with beautiful wild mushrooms, produce or cheese.

We are seeing more and more talented people drawn to the Okanagan than ever before. The climate, the produce and the amazing wines produced within the valley are attracting people here. We as chefs will continue to hone our craft and push each other to become stronger. All I can hope for is the continued support of the people who live here. It's the locals and the regular customers that keep our restaurants flourishing!"

THE FARMER

Helen Kennedy, Arlo's Honey Farm, Kelowna

With a philosophy that healthy bees are happy bees, this small bee farm in South Kelowna has heart.

In her own words:
"We meet many people here throughout the year, and while they all like honey, they are amazed when they learn about the many obstacles bees face in their existence, how many bees it takes to create their jar of honey and the impact the loss of the bee would have on the food chain world wide. The bees seem to be insignificant to the majority. Possibly because they are small insects instead of being cute and cuddly? The harm and damage done to bees somehow is not considered the same as animals. For example when cattle, horses or pets are starved to death, it is a major crime. If a beekeeper neglects or starves his or her hives over the winter - no one notices. I give kudos to the Boys & Girls Clubs, the 4 H Groups, and the SPCA summer camps for bringing their groups to our farm to educate the children about honeybees. I am seeing a shift in my consumer base to younger clientele. This I attribute mainly to the movement of eating healthy and eating raw food. The movement away from GMO altered products has many consumers replacing white sugar (GMO sugar beets) with honey, because honey unlike stevia or other substitutes does not have to be processed and is the only food that does not spoil. Honey has significant health benefits and properties that go way beyond being just a sweetener and these younger more health conscious consumers are doing their research and making the connection."

THE WINEMAKER

Jeff Martin, La Frenz Winery, Naramata

Australian born Jeff Martin's passion for sustainable vineyard practices is inspiring. Jeff became involved in the wine industry at the age of eighteen, when he was employed by renowned Australian producer McWilliams as a trainee winemaker at their half million case Beelbangera facility. Years later, in 1989, Jeff became the chief red winemaker for the McWilliams group, with his wines winning major awards at Australian wine shows.

Following a sabbatical in Napa, he and his wife Niva stopped over to see the Okanagan Valley and fell in love – they moved here in 1994.

Jeff has built an almost self-sustainable ecosystem with his Naramata properties using Mother Nature as his vineyard manager.

In His Own Words:
"It's about creating diversity in our vineyard environment, the opposite to modern farming monocultures where specializing in single crops and animals has created an overdependence on fossil fuels and a depletion of our resources. Farmers compensate by adding fertilizers and nutrients when nature and natural processes do a much better job of it."

To fertilize his vineyards, Jeff has employed over a hundred chickens, a few cows, some sheep who also help with pruning and of course mowing. Jeff feels that "in the truest sense of the word, the full environment – the terroir – not just winemaking techniques and types of yeast, or barrels, potentially most influences the quality and unique expression of our wines."

La Frenz's wine portfolio has won an impressive list of awards and offers a range of beautiful wines including fortified wines with an impressive Port.

PAIRING

La Frenz LV Liqueur Muscat

This wine is produced in a traditional solera system, meaning the average age of the blend is getting progressively older. Every year's release has a percentage of their first vintage in 1999. It has beautiful flavors of caramelized brown sugar, cinnamon, Muscat fruit with that lovely sweet, power and complexity that can only come from time.

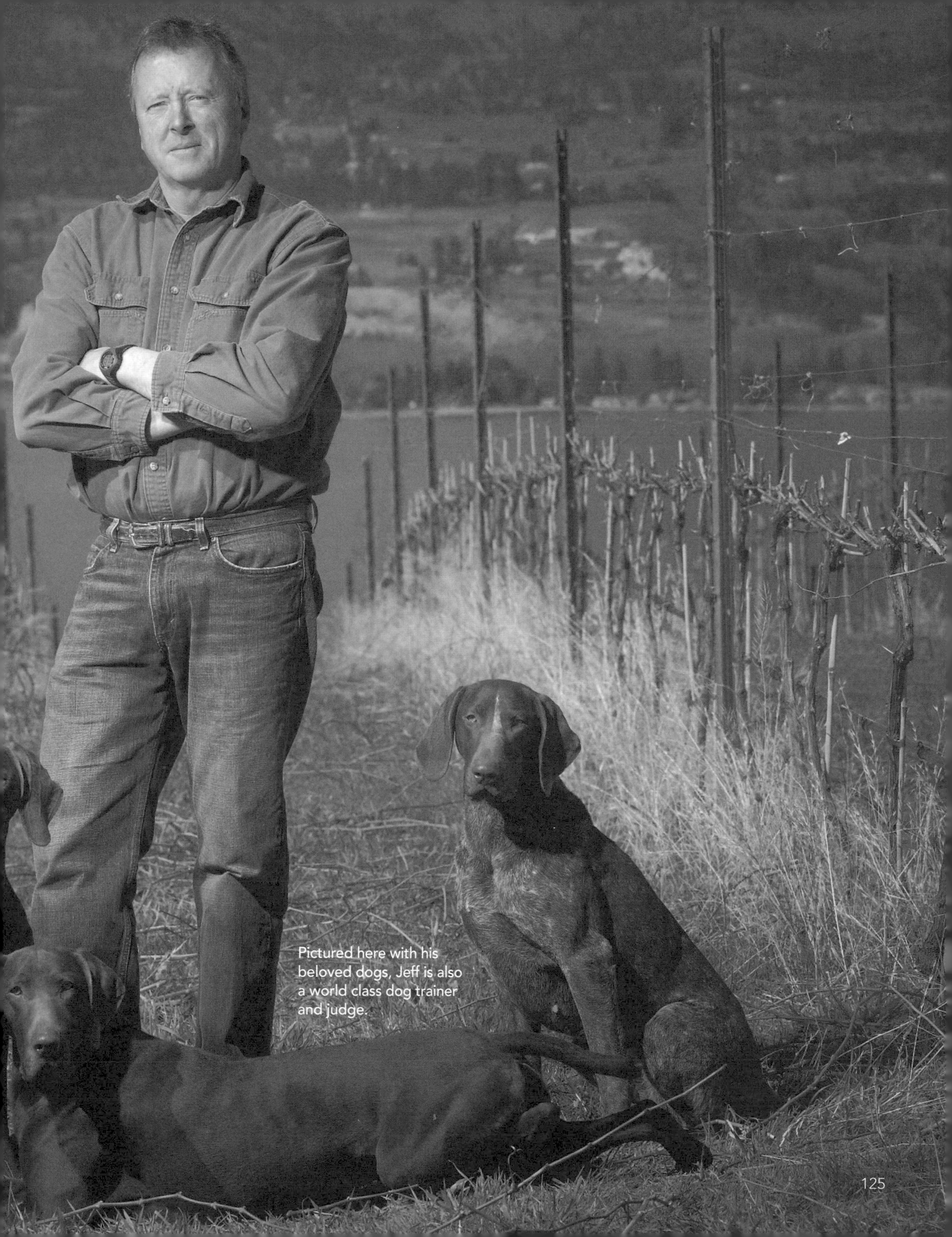

Pictured here with his beloved dogs, Jeff is also a world class dog trainer and judge.

OKANAGAN LAVENDER MASCARPONE SOUFFLE

CHEF: JENNA PILLON, LOCAL LOUNGE • GRILLE, SUMMERLAND
FARMER: ANDREA MCFADDEN, OKANAGAN LAVENDER FARM, KELOWNA
WINEMAKER: SLEEPING GIANT WINERY, SUMMERLAND

A beautiful dreamlike setting awaits you at the Okanagan Lavender Farm. Follow the intoxicating scent of these famously French purple flowers around to the back of their farm shop and be rewarded with a haze of purple flowers backdropped onto Okanagan Lake. Culinary lavender is such a lovely, versatile cooking ingredient and is available in the farm store.

Ganache:
270g milk chocolate
105g whipping cream
21g butter (room tempature)
50g walnuts, toasted (rough chop)

Melt chocolate in medium bowl over water on medium heat. Bring cream to simmer. Add cream to chocolate and put in to tall skinny container. Buzz with hand blender until just combined, add butter. Buzz until combined, tap container on counter to get air out of ganache. Let cool for 5 minutes, put in to piping bag and put into desired mould, rimmed with acetate. Cover the top with walnuts. Put in cooler for 30 minutes then let set at room temperature for 2 hours.

Graham Cracker:
3 oz soft butter
1.35 oz brown sugar
55 oz icing sugar
1 tsp ground cinnamon
¼ tsp cloves
3.5 oz flour
1/4 tsp baking soda
1/8 tsp salt

Cream butter, sugars, cinnamon, cloves. Add flour, baking soda, salt to creamed mixture. Stir together till combined (cool/rest in fridge for 30 min.) Roll out on floured surface to 1/8 of an inch thick, cut desired shapes and bake at 375ºF for 7-9 minutes.

Lemon Curd:
77ml lemon juice
1.5 whole eggs
½ egg yolk
85g white sugar
113g cubed butter
pinch salt

Bring 2 inches of water in a pot to a simmer. Combine lemon juice, whole eggs, ½ egg yolk, sugar and salt in a stainless steel bowl, whisk immediately. Sit bowl over pot of water, whisk together. Stir constantly till very thick (180ºF) 10 to 12 minutes. Let cool to 140ºF and put in to a blender. One at a time, add butter cubes to cooked mixture (don't add more until other butter is combined.) Pour into insert, cool in fridge.

Lavender Mascarpone :
soufflé 4 eggs (separated)
30g sugar
100g mascarpone
3 sprigs of lavender
zest of one lemon
metal moulds (2 inch diameter, 3 inch high)

Set oven to 400ºF. Cut out tin foil and fold around the bottom of your cylinder; mould tightly 3/4 of the way up (covered bottom, open top). Brush bottom and sides of mould with melted butter and coat with sugar. Set moulds in baking dishes (must hold ½ inch of water). In a large bowl put 4 egg whites. In a medium bowl put 4 egg yolks. In a medium bowl put mascarpone, lavender and zest.

Whisk egg yolks with 0.5oz of sugar till light and fluffy, mix into mascarpone and zest. Whisk egg whites and 0.5oz of sugar with clean dry whisk until soft peaks. In 3 parts fold egg yolk mixture into egg whites. Fill moulds with soufflé mix. Cover bottom of baking pan with ½ inch of water. Bake for 14 minutes. Remove from oven, let rest for 2 minutes. Then carefully remove from moulds. Use an off set metal spatula to transfer soufflés.

Strawberry Essence:
300g strawberries, sliced
50g sugar
15ml lemon juice

Combine all ingredients in a pot. Cook until strawberries are soft and liquid has reduced a quarter. Puree in a blender. Pass mixture through fine strainer. Cool.

Lavender Sugar:
100g sugar
5 sprigs of dried lavender

Combine ingredients together.

Vanilla Bean Berry Salad
170g blackberries, halved
170g raspberries, halved
1 vanilla bean
20 g sugar

Cut vanilla bean in half, scrape out the inside of bean. Stir together all ingredients slowly. Let the berries macerate in the sugar.
Enjoy!

THE CHEF

Jenna Pillon, Local Lounge • Grille, Summerland

Jenna Pillon started her career out with a bang after winning the 2012 Junior Chef of the Year at the National Chefs Conference in Halifax. Her three-course winning meal included a version of the dessert she has chosen to share with us. Now working under Chef Paul Cecconi at Local Lounge • Grille, after her win she expressed gratitude by explaining, "The support of the Okanagan Chefs Association and Local were instrumental in helping me hone my culinary techniques. A huge thank you to Chef Cecconi and Chef Casavant who have coached me in so many of the practical kitchen skills needed and influenced me with their inventive and inspired cooking." Recently becoming Mrs. Jenna Pillon (nee Angle), Jenna married another local Chef, Brent Pillon, Chef at Hillside Winery Bistro in Naramata. What a delicious couple!

THE FARMER

Andrea McFadden, Okanagan Lavender & Herb Farm, Kelowna

Owner Andrea McFadden and her husband David have created a beautiful oasis on their lake view property. Rows of lavender run down the property interspersed with herb plants – making this farm a sensory experience. Lavender is believed to aid a multitude of problems, including stress, anxiety, headaches, insomnia, depression, colds, upset stomach and nervousness. Its intoxicating scent can be distilled into essential oil and used as perfume or used medicinally when inhaled to induce relaxation and sleep and ease stress. As a culinary herb, the scent and taste will transform the most ordinary dish into the extraordinary. Because of its unique flavour, the addition of lavender adds a certain mystique and visually, its just so darn pretty.

Andrea also gives a lot back to the community through education. As daughter of pioneer winery owner Dick Stewart of Quails' Gate Winery, Andrea has farming in her soul. She loves to host children's workshops and introduce them to exciting new flavours and "teach them where food comes from. I want them to learn something useful and easy" such as showing them how to make a salad dressing or tea.

In her own words:
"Our Irish grandfather arrived in the Okanagan in 1908. He paved the way for his descendants to embrace agriculture as a way of life, first working for David Gellatly at the historic Gellatly Nut Farm on the Westside and then starting Stewart Brothers Nursery in Kelowna in 1911. Formerly an apple orchard, the farm now grows over 60 varieties of lavender and also has a u-pick bed to experience the joie de vivre of harvesting this soothing plant."

THE WINEMAKER

Sleeping Giant Fruit Winery, Summerland

Sleeping Giant Fruit Winery is owned by Okanagan jam and syrup makers, Summerland Sweets. Mr. F.E. (Ted) Atkinson founded Summerland Sweets in 1962 and since then it has been a destination for visitors and locals who love sweet. Atkinson's dedication to preserving local fruits has won him longevity in this dying business. The Okanagan was filled with canneries and fruit processing plants from the late 1800's up to the 1960's when they began to disappear due to big corporate buy ups. A lesson in sustainability Summerland Sweets not only creates jams, syrups and brittles – they also utilize our local bounty in wines.

Fruit Winemaker Ron Taylor has a degree in Microbiology from the University of British Columbia.

PAIRING

Sleeping Giant Raspberry Fruit Wine

A glass full of raspberry essence and a 2 in sweetness, this wine is a berry good match for the mascarpone soufflé.

PEACH TIRAMISU

CHEF: RICARDO SCEBBA, RICARDO'S MEDITERRANEAN KITCHEN, LAKE COUNTRY
FARMER: TOM THOMPSON, LAKE COUNTRY CULINARY FARMS, LAKE COUNTRY
WINEMAKER: FORBIDDEN FRUIT WINERY, SIMILKAMEEN

In this gorgeous twist on the traditional Italian version of Tiramisu, Ricardo utilizes the fruit in season from his neighbourhood. Raspberries, strawberries, apricots or peaches - this dessert is easy and is a hit whatever version you make. Buon appetito!

SERVES 10-12

Ingredients:

250 ml jar peach preserves
1/3 cup plus 4 tbsp peach schnapps
1/3 cup peach juice or mango juice nectar
500 g mascarpone cheese, room temperature
1 -1/3 cup whipping cream
1/3 cup sugar
1 tsp vanilla extract
36 ladyfingers (savoiardi)
4 peaches, skins removed, sliced into small pieces

9x12 glass or Pyrex dish

In a bowl, mix preserves, 1/3 cup peach schnapps, peach juice or mango nectar, set aside.
In another bowl, mix mascarpone plus remaining peach schnapps together with spatula. In a mixer whip cream, sugar, vanilla to firm peaks. Combine cream mixture into mascarpone mixture and fold or whisk until smooth. Take half of the preserve mixture and cover bottom of pan. Place 18 ladyfingers side by side over preserves. Sprinkle half the peaches over ladyfingers. Cover with half of mascarpone cream mixture. Repeat a second layer. Cover and chill for 2 or more hours or overnight. Place fresh sliced peaches over portion when serving.
Buon appetito!

Chef Ricardo Scebba (L)
with Tom Thompson

THE CHEF

Ricardo Scebba, Ricardo's Mediterranean Kitchen, Lake Country

Ricardo has gone from being a chef running a busy restaurant with a big family at home to a chef with a best-selling cookbook, a TV cooking show co-hosted with his wife and partner Sue Miller, an even busier restaurant and bigger family at home. Never a dull moment in the Scebba-Miller world. Over the last couple of years, with their success doubling, the couple has been integrating their children into the business hoping that they may be able to retire one day. Although, looking at Ricardo's parents Connie and Joe Scebba who are still very much involved with their son's business, from sharing recipes, rolling meatballs and growing vegetables, I think this is a life-long gig. But they seem to thrive on it – Sue is never without a big smile and a joke and Ricardo comes alive when entertaining his guests, including new Grand-baby Bo. That is amore.

Sue and Ricardo use as much local ingredients as possible and take a green-friendly approach to running their restaurant for which they received a Green Business Award in 2011. For music aficionados, their Thursday jazz nights are fantastic.

Basically, every time you leave Ricardo's you feel like you have just been to a big Italian family wedding.

THE FARMER

Tom Thompson, Lake Country Culinary Farms, Lake Country

A former chef and food wholesaler, Tom Thompson knows a lot about food and what chefs are looking for. He, his wife Donella and sister Lil operate their vegetable (and flower) farm in beautiful Lake Country located between Kelowna and Vernon. With a beautiful array of special vegetables and herbs to choose from including: red carrots, candy striped beets, Russian blue potatoes, golden turnips, rainbow chard, yellow and green patty pans, cheddar cauliflower, orange banana tomatoes, pink banana squash, chocolate mint, mauve lavender, purple ruffled basil, black raspberries (just to name a few) - it is no wonder they are a favorite supplier of some of the Okanagan's finest restaurants.

In his own words:
"We have certainly noticed a difference since we started our farming careers. Restauranteurs, chefs and the public are much more accepting of the idea of local produce actually grown in their immediate neighborhoods, not a hundred (or more) miles away... some even seeking it out. We were on the cutting edge of this concept and have worked hard to promote it to the culinary trade and the general public. There are many more small farms growing and selling a variety of veggies to both restaurants and the public through farmgate and farmers' markets, as well as direct sales. In the future, we will continue to work with our chefs to develop menus that truly take the best advantage of using a variety of vegetables throughout the season. Not having a particular vegetable written into the menu, but rather being flexible so as to incorporate what is available that week/day. We will also continue to educate and promote what to look for in a high quality product and how to best keep it top quality."

THE WINEMAKER

Forbidden Fruit Winery, Similkameen

Nestled on the banks of the Similkameen River, this 142-acre organic farm is a modern day Garden of Eden – an apropos description and also inspiration for their name, Forbidden Fruit! Kim Brind'Amour and Steve Venables started Ven'Amour Organic Farms in 1981 and are celebrating a record 35 years of organic farming. "Ven 'Amour Organic Farms has been farmed organically since day one, in 1977. The farm was Certified Organic in 1984, the year certification began in BC."
These pioneer organic farmers are a family-run operation and have over 65 varieties of tree fruits plus the new addition of grapevines. Their wide variety of award-winning fruit wines have been a phenomenal success. The Earth Series of grape wines are the responsibility of Steve's son Nathan Venables who is "slowly taking over much of the grape winemaking duties at Forbidden Fruit".

PAIRING

Crushed Innocence – White Peach Dessert Wine

This pairing is absolutely peachy! Crafted from 100% white fleshed organic peaches, this beautiful elixir is delicate yet still packs a flavour bomb of summer essence in each sip.

Pepper Strawberry & Cream Pavlova w/Balsamic Vinegar

CHEFS: ANNINA AND JÖRG HOFFMEISTER, DOLCI RESTAURANT & CATERING, OSOYOOS
VINEGAR MAKER: ALOIS THURN, OKANAGAN VINEGAR BREWERY, SUMMERLAND
WINEMAKER: THE VIEW WINERY, KELOWNA

This dessert is beautiful and elegant. The individual servings begin with a crunch and end with a surprising, creamy middle. The balsamic vinegar on the plate adds a lovely zip and topping the dish with fresh flowers, like Annina did, will make you a star at your dinner party.

Pavlova:
4 egg whites, room temperature
(save 4 egg yolks for Vanilla Cream below)
140 g sugar
1/2 tsp white vinegar

Beat in mixer until hard peaks form.

Add and carefully fold in:
60 g sugar
10 g corn starch, sifted
Juice from one lemon

Load into piping bag and with a No 12 pipe, draw circles on baking sheet and make little nests (or use a spoon.)
Bake at 215ºC for about 1 hour. Turn oven off and let sit for 2 more hours. Can be made in advance and kept in air tight container at room temperature.

Vanilla Cream:
Slowly heat up:
400 ml milk
50 grams sugar
Seeds of 1/2 vanilla bean and bean
4 egg yolks

Plus:
200 ml heavy cream (36%)
2 oz Grand Marnier

Slightly whisk 4 egg yolks up in a bowl. Add milk little at time to temper. Pour back into saucepan and carefully boil until thickened. Pour through strainer and cover tightly with wrap. Place in fridge to cool.
Carefully wash strawberries and cut into quarters. Place in bowl. Add 2 oz of Grand Marnier and some freshly ground pepper. Let soak for about 2 hours.
Whip heavy cream until soft peaks form. Fold in Vanilla Cream and 2 oz of Grand Marnier. Place cream mixture on top of Pavlovas, top with strawberries and garnish with icing sugar sprinkled fresh lemon balm and small dots of aged balsamic vinegar from Okanagan Vinegar Brewery to your liking.

Annina (L) & Jörg with daughter Jennifer

THE CHEFS

Annina and Jörg Hoffmeister, Dolci Restaurant & Catering, Osoyoos

Dolci Deli & Catering Proprietors, Chefs, Chocolatiers and husband and wife, Annina and Jörg Hoffmeister moved to Canada in 1997 to pursue their dream of owning a bakery/restaurant. Talk about the ultimate foodies, this couple does everything from creating wedding cakes to mouthwatering charcuterie. Both received their degrees in Europe – she in Switzerland and he in Germany – and have brought us their creative talents and passion plus their worldly scope of flavours and tastes.

Annina and Jörg focus their menu on fresh local produce and offer a local wine list featuring many of their award-winning neighbours. Also a successful catering business in the South Okanagan, Dolci's name will be seen at many large functions and winery events in Oliver and Osoyoos.

In Annina's own words:
"When we moved to the Okanagan, we were thrilled with the large and wide variety of orchards. Never have we had a peach where the juice just sprayed out all over you and you need to hold it with two hands. Back in Europe they were much smaller and hard like an apple. We were always cooking seasonal and fresh and we just knew that this was one of the many things this area had to offer.

It is incredible to see what has happened here over the past decade. With only a few places to have dinner at when we first got here (Osoyoos), there weren't too many nights out. It wasn't that the places weren't good but there weren't many to choose from. Now, however, it is great to see all the diverse food that new restaurants have to offer. We could go out to a different place every night and know we're going to enjoy a fabulous meal.

One of our favorite Okanagan meals is a simple salad with heirloom tomatoes, grilled peaches and local cheese, topped with fresh basil and Okanagan aged balsamic with an artisan baguette on the side.

What do you see or wish for the future here? I think we are on the right track. It matters more to us what we eat, where it comes from and how is it grown. We believe that if it grows together, it goes together."

THE VINEGAR MAKER

Alois Thurn, Okanagan Vinegar Brewery, Summerland

Alois Thurn moved to Canada in 1982 from Marmagen, Germany, an agricultural region near Cologne. With a rich history in family farming – traceable back to 1117 (also the name on his new wine label) – the creation of food runs deep in his blood.

Alois has always worked in the food industry; he is a trained sausage-maker and has consulted on various industry levels. His excellent palate and industrious nature lead him into the exciting world of vinegar brewing. Because the creation of true vinegars, like his rich and delicious balsamico, need years to age, just like a fine wine, Thurn has had time to follow other projects like buying and planting a vineyard. Now, with a 27,000 case production in house – his vinegar is better than ever and he has recently completed his first crush for new wine label: 1117-Thurn. He will be introducing a Gewürztraminer, Pinot Gris and Pinot Noir, all Estate-grown, to our wine world.

Thurn also imports beautiful olive oil from the South Andalusia region of Spain from a small family estate. His product line now includes five categories: wine vinegars, fruit vinegars, balsamic vinegars, wine jellies and condiments. His wine vinegars include a sherry wine, Riesling white wine and Champagne vinegar, and the fruit vinegars are black cherry, raspberry and apple. The intense and gorgeous Solera 2000 is a rich Pinot Noir balsamico that has been aged in the barrique style (Bordeaux barrels) for six years.

THE WINEMAKER

The View Winery, Kelowna

Jennifer Turton-Molgat

Stylish "Head Diva" at The View Winery Jennifer Turton-Molgat comes from a rich local history of tree fruit farming going back five generations. The View's tasting room, located on Ward Road in Kelowna, is actually the original packinghouse built by Great Granddad Ward in 1922. Jen says, "These rich and fruitful lands have been nurtured by the Wards/ Turtons since the initial plantings by my Great-Grandfather George Ward in the early 1920's. The View from Block 12 Riesling is my favourite." In keeping with their unique brand, there lies mystique in the sexy, head turning label – a red high heel shoe corking a bottle of wine. That red shoe has now become their trademark with Head Diva Jennifer wearing it well. She tells the story: "Well, we went dancing. We danced until my red pumps started to pinch. We went home and finished a bottle of Merlot. He (husband Kent) playfully removed my shoes and stuffed the heel of one shoe into the empty bottle... and there it was, with an overturned glass beside it, an image of our own making, spoke to us our love of wine, born by accident during a fun and carefree moment..."

Winemaker Andrew Shillington joined the team at The View in 2009.

PAIRING

2011 Distraction Frizzante

Tiny bubbles tickle your nose as they explode in a symphony of Okanagan berries. Fresh and crisp, this sparkling wine pairs well with a summer barbecue and dancing bare foot in the orchard.

QUINCE & CHOCOLATE TARTE

CHEF/BAKER: MONIKA WALKER, OKANAGAN GROCERY ARTISAN BREADS, KELOWNA
FARMER: DAVID O'NEIL, O'NEIL ORCHARDS, WEST KELOWNA
COFFEE MICRO ROASTERS: DEB SYNNOT AND JOHN ANDERSON, BEAN SCENE COFFEE HOUSE, KELOWNA

There is not a person on this planet who doesn't melt into some minor state of Nirvana after walking into a room smelling of freshly baked bread. Like some sort of happiness makers, bakers hold a place of honour on the list of positive contributors to life.
Monika also creates amazing dessert treats like crème brûlée and her iconic Bernard Callebaut Chocolate Bread. These beautiful tarts are a delicious celebration of the unique flavour of quince.

1 batch = approx. 12- 4″ inch tarts

Sugar Pastry:
200 g butter, room temperature
200 g sugar
100 g egg, whisked slightly
400 g pastry flour, sifted
* make sure all ingredients are at room temperature

Cream together butter and sugar just until well incorporated. Add eggs a little at a time until well mixed then add all of the flour all at once and mix until blended - do not over mix. Chill for at least 1 hour or overnight.

Quince Curd:
2 1/2 cups quince
1/4 cup butter
1/4 cup sugar
2 oranges, zest and juice
1 ml salt

Zest oranges, set aside zest for ganache, then juice oranges and reserve. Rub fuzz off quince (approx. 3 pieces of fruit) and poach quince in water till tender, cool and chop roughly. Sauté quince in a little butter add sugar, salt & orange juice. Reduce liquid by half, puree and add rest of butter.

Orange Ganache:
250 g dark chocolate
250 g 35% heavy cream
2 oranges (zest)
30 ml rum

Chop chocolate and place in bowl, set aside. Heat cream till scalding (just before boil), pour over chocolate and let sit 5 minutes. Add zest and rum, blend into ganache.

Candied Quince:
1 quince
1 cup sugar
1/2 cup water
1 cup sugar for coating

Rub fuzz off quince and poach in water till tender, cool and chop into 1/4 "inch pieces. Place water in saucepan, add sugar and bring to boil. Add quince and heat to 230ºF using candy thermometer. Strain through sieve - and toss in extra sugar and cool, toss in sugar again.

Assembly:
Preheat oven to 350ºF.
Scale 45 g sugar party per tart shell, form into balls, then roll out 1/8th inch thick rounds and place in tart shell, pierce with fork for even baking.
Refrigerate for 5 - 10 minutes then bake at 350ºF until golden (10 - 12 minutes) - cool.
Spread approx 3 tbsp quince curd into tart shell, pour warm ganache over quince curd and chill till set (15 minutes). Place 1 - 3 pieces of candied quince on top of ganache in the centre of the tart and dive in!

THE CHEF/BAKER

Monika Walker, Okanagan Grocery Artisan Breads, Kelowna

Okanagan Grocery Artisan Breads in Kelowna is owned and operated by Monika Walker or "Monika The Baker" (her email handle) and her husband Bill. Her breads are all made with organic unbleached local white flour, most with a natural starter (named Naomi) and are hand-shaped and baked. "We do not add any strange fats or products to bulk up the size of the loaves, making the breads as naturally as possible." As well as good breads and baked goods, Monika and Bill are stocking other locally inspired and created treats in their turquoise hued shop. Monika's second bakeshop opened up this year on Windsor Road in Kelowna with addition of the drip coffee bar to savour with a treat. Customers are now able to inhale the mood enhancing fragrance of fresh bread baking and coffee while they shop - ohmmmm. Ring cowbell for service.

In her own words:
"The Okanagan was love at first sight - irresistibly beautiful countryside with the best produce I have ever tasted.
I see more and more emerging artisans, the next generation of our community going back to the basics of canning our wonderful seasonal produce, making their own bread and cooking seasonally, organically and sustainably. Okanagan cuisine is a small pond of culinary treasures that are waiting to be discovered. We shop at our local farmers' market in the summertime, process, can and preserve fruit for our bakery in the summer to supply us all winter. It is wonderful to know the farmers and their families and to support them directly."

THE FARMER

David O'Neil, O'Neil Orchards, West Kelowna

David O'Neil is a unique supplier to local chefs – he grows quince! Located in Lakeview Heights in West Kelowna, David inherited his quince orchard of 400 trees from his father-in-law Peter Pearson 30 years ago. The pear quince and apple quince varieties that he grows are hard to find and are a favorite to the culinary industry.

What the heck is quince? Quince is a funny looking fruit. Somewhat homely, they are yellow, lumpy, covered in fuzz and are terribly sour when eaten raw. However, they are very aromatic and when cooked or made into preserves, they are a heavenly treat.

David doesn't spray and only feeds them calcium which he says, "the old trees love." His crop yields from 10,000 to 12,000 pounds with some of the quince weighing in at a healthy 2 1/2 pounds each. David tenderly picks the entire crop himself as they are extremely delicate and they bruise easily. He describes harvesting quince like "picking eggs."

Monika and David were introduced through Chef Rod Butters at RauDZ and have enjoyed a quince-a-full relationship ever since.

Quince make fantastic jams and jellies but David says his favorite is to "slice them in half, sprinkle with brown sugar and cinnamon, bake them and serve with vanilla ice cream."

COFFEE MICRO-ROASTER

Deb Synnot and John Anderson, Bean Scene Coffee House, Kelowna

Deb Synnot and John Anderson, "Kelowna's Coffee Power Couple," moved here 10 years ago from the Coast and their former lives: she a nurse, and he in waterworks construction. They bought the Bean Scene downtown and their love affair with brewing the bean began. They operate three shops in Kelowna, one with an in-house roastery.

In her own words:
"John was lucky enough to be taught by Patrick Graf (our espresso is called Espresso Graf in honour of him). Patrick was the first micro-roaster in Vancouver; he sold his company to what is now JJ Bean. His conditions were simple, that we roast old school – small batch (we have a 20 kg roaster) and no computer programming to guide roasting. Over time we have changed our roasting style to put a greater emphasis on the inherent flavour a green bean brings to the table. Much like grapes, all the conditions in which they are grown and then processed affect the green bean taste. Therefore all of our medium roasts are a single origin (one bean from one place). We use a couple of green bean suppliers that specialize in sustainability through buying from single estate farms. In addition we have maintained small batch, artisan style and on demand roasting only (we do not roast until coffee is ordered, no roasted coffee is stored for future use). We have embraced the "keep it simple" approach throughout all we do in our business – let the ingredients speak."

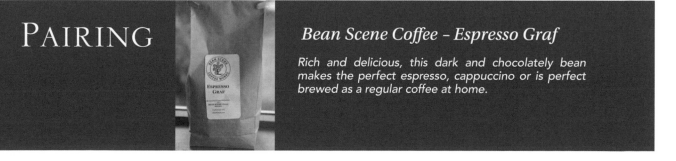

PAIRING

Bean Scene Coffee – Espresso Graf

Rich and delicious, this dark and chocolately bean makes the perfect espresso, cappuccino or is perfect brewed as a regular coffee at home.

SIMILKAMEEN CRAB APPLES BAKED IN LOCAL HONEY w/ CANADOS ICE CREAM

CHEFS: RHYS PENDER AND ALISHAN DRIEDIGER, CAWSTON
SPIRITMAKER: OKANAGAN SPIRITS, KELOWNA
WINEMAKER: STONEBOAT WINERY, OLIVER

This dessert is a celebration of local Similkameen cuisine. The crab apples are from Rhys and Alishan's own (monstrous) 100-year-old tree on their farm. The classic French apple brandy Calvados ice cream is localized by using Okanagan Spirits' Canados brandy. Alishan says that she first tasted this easy-peasy ice cream at Rhys' Aunt's in New Zealand and since then it has become "a family favorite"- daughters Madeline (not pictured) and Elodie (left) can testify to that!

Apples:
12-14 crab apples - enough to cover (when halved) bottom of an 8 x 10 Pyrex dish. If you don't have a 100-year-old crab apple tree, ours produces about 2 tons every other year so come and help yourself.
Approximately 4 tablespoons local honey - your favourite (we use Similkameen Apiaries from Cawston or also available at the Penticton Farmers Market)

Ice Cream:
1 can sweetened condensed milk
whipping cream - 500ml - something thick like local Avalon Dairy
Okanagan Spirits Canados - 2 tablespoons (you can substitute your favourite spirit)
honeycomb or toasted almonds (optional) - chopped to add texture to ice cream

Method:
Easiest ice cream you will ever make! Make in advance. Whip cream until stiff peaks form. Add tin of sweetened condensed milk and Canados and fold in to whipped cream. Fold in honeycomb or almonds if using. Pour mixture into container (Tupperware or glass works well), cover with cling film and put in freezer until firm (approximately 8 hours).

Apples:
Chop crab apples in half vertically.
Using melon baller or small spoon, remove core.
Place halves of crab apple in Pyrex dish.
Drizzle with honey then toss to coat apples.
Spread apples evenly over base with cut side down.
Roast in oven at 350ºF until apples are soft and honey starts to caramelize, approximately 50-55 minutes or until juices are golden.
Can drizzle juices from pan over top.

Serve honey baked apples topped with scoops of ice cream. Simple and tasty and local.

The Chefs

Rhys Pender and Alishan Driediger, Cawston

Husband and wife dream team Rhys Pender and Alishan Driediger are an extraordinary combination of the best of our food and wine world. Both Chefs (Rhys also became Canada's 4th Master of Wine in 2010!) the couple opened Okanagan Grocery - Artisan Breads in 2003 (now owned by Monika Walker). Now settled with their two young girls on a vineyard in the Similkameen, they recently released their first vintage of wine under the Little Farm label.

In their own words:
"We moved up to the Okanagan following a passion for wine. It probably started in France when we spent the summer in Avignon and Aix-en-Provence and discovered a passion for great food. That was in 1996. We moved to Canada in 1997. In 1998 we both completed a Professional Culinary Program at Dubrulle Hotel & Culinary Institute where we honed our love of food into real skills. In 2003 we were able to move back to the Okanagan permanently. We started baking bread for the farmers' markets in Kelowna and Penticton and finally opened our

bakery at Guisachan Village. We bought our five acre plot in Cawston in 2008.
The Similkameen is like a less moneyed version of the Okanagan but the potential is enormous and there are so many great characters. But it is really the quality of the food and the fact that so much of it is organic that makes it such a great place to live and cook. We can grow practically anything here.
The Similkameen is unique because it's very beautiful, the soils are very complex and there is the persistent wind that cleans everything up and makes it ideal for organic production. These elements make for great wine growing as well as intensely flavoured fruits and vegetables. There really is an amazing bounty available in such a small area. What is developing (Okanagan cuisine) is very multi-dimensional as the top chefs who are behind it are bringing a diverse range of cuisines and cooking styles and applying those using the fantastic local ingredients. Things like the salmon run out of Osoyoos Lake, local trout and venison are great and it would be great to see locally raised duck and rabbit as these are easy to farm. "

THE STILLMASTER

Okanagan Spirits, Kelowna

The Okanagan Spirits story is a lesson in innovation and sustainability. Original owner and Still Master Frank Dieter was inspired to utilize the leftover tree fruits discarded after harvest for being damaged or those left to rot on the ground following weather damage or neglect. Another old world principle in action – sort of like "if life gives you lemons… make lemonade." Well, life gave Frank apples, apricots, pears, cherries and more so he made spirits.

The original distillery remains in Vernon with a second location downtown Kelowna opened by new owners the Dyck family. The range of spirits created is fantastic and their repertoire even includes the fabled Absinthe made from wormwood.

Frank Dieter now operates a mobile juicing factory that will come to your farm or co-op of neighbouring farms to crush and bottle your fruit into fresh pure nutritious pasteurized apple juice. Genius.

The French have Calvados – we have Canados. Okanagan

Still Master Peter von Hahn

Spirits' Canados is mainly distilled from Hyslop Crab Apples and offers lively flavors of exotic fruit and cinnamon with hints of oak and vanilla.

THE WINEMAKER

Stoneboat Vineyards, Oliver

The Martinuik family is not new to the vineyard business – they were growing award-winning grapes for 23 years before they created their first vintage in 2005 and shortly thereafter opened their own winery 2007.

In their own words:

Jay Martinuik, Winemaker & Viticulture - "We make our wines to pair with food- the two together enhance the sensory experience. When we're deciding upon final blends, the family always puts them to the test at dinner."

Tim Martinuik (the family foodie), General Manager, Marketing & Grounds Keeping - "I keep honeybees and grow heirloom tomatoes, Cape gooseberries and edamame beans right next to a row of Pinot Noir, and all of them, grapes & bees included, thrive because of the sun and heat."

Alison Moyes (L) and Tim Martiniuk

Lanny Martiniuk, Proprietor & Dad - "We like to talk about what is beneath under our soils- rocks. Our vineyards on the Lower Black Sage grow in a couple feet of soil over 100+ feet of stones that are frosted with calcium. It's hard to farm, but our Pinots love it."

Winemaker Alison Moyes - "There is an unmistakable mineral quality to our wines that we attribute to the calcium on our rocks. We also have very hot days and very cool nights, which brings lush fruit and freshness to our whites and reds. You can only find these qualities in a tiny area of Oliver - Osoyoos - it's one example of the many, many microclimates and soil types packed into the valley, which is so small compared to other wine regions."

PAIRING

2010 Stoneboat Verglas

Spice, honey and orange zest on the nose with a lovely hint of acidity that rolls onto your palate with a beautiful blend of stone fruits and citrus.

Trembling Ehrenfelser Jelly

**CHEF: GEOFFREY COUPER, INSTRUCTOR OKANAGAN COLLEGE CULINARY ARTS/
CHAIRMAN OKANAGAN CHEFS ASSOCIATION, KELOWNA
FARMER: ROGER BORRETT, KELOWNA
WINEMAKER: CEDARCREEK ESTATE WINERY, KELOWNA**

This beautiful dessert will evoke gasps from your guests. This glistening, jiggling – or shall we say trembling – work of art is easy to make and it replicates looking through a stained glass window. It also wraps up the wine and produce of the Okanagan into one delicious package.

Ingredients:
500 ml white grape juice
500 ml Ehrenfelser wine (local suggestion:
CedarCreek Ehrenfelser)
11 gelatin leaves
500 g fresh assorted Okanagan berries

Yields approximately 12 – 90 ml timbale molds.

Method:
Begin this recipe a day ahead. Soak the gelatin leaves in 750 ml of cold water for 5 minutes to soften. Meanwhile, warm half [250 ml] of the white grape juice over low heat in a small pot. Squeeze the excess water from the gelatin leaves then add them to the warm grape juice. Stir to dissolve.
Now add the Ehrenfelser wine and the remainder of the grape juice. Cool the mixture slightly.
Pour 30 ml of the mixture into each mold. Chill until set in the cooler, approximately 30 minutes. Once set add 30 grams of the berries to each mold. Cool the remaining jelly mix until it has the texture of egg whites, then pour over the berries and fill the container to just below the top. Return to the cooler and allow to set up overnight.
To serve, briefly dip each mold into hot water to loosen, then turn out onto pre-chilled dessert plates. Garnish with the remaining berries and a fruit purée, crème fraiche or thick yogurt as desired. TADA!

THE CHEF

Geoffrey Couper, Instructor Okanagan College Culinary Arts

Current Chairman of the Okanagan Chefs Association, Culinary Apprenticeship Instructor, wine lover and raconteur extraordinaire are just a few of the toques that "Cheffrey" wears.

With three decades of award winning experience behind him the obsession for great food, simply prepared with passionately produced local products only burns brighter.

Having called Kelowna home for over 10 years he has had the opportunity to provide culinary inspiration for many great wine producers in the valley including Mission Hill, CedarCreek, Blue Mountain and Andrew Peller amongst others.

His advice to all young chefs looking for education and inspiration? Go work on a farm. After a classic apprenticeship Geoffrey departed to Europe to do the typical travel, eat and work thing, at the time thinking he knew a fair bit about cooking. Ending up on a small family farm in southern Germany what the young culinarian soon realized was that he knew nothing about food. And there is a huge difference between the two. "To see products destined for the table being raised, weeded, milked, vinified, to witness firsthand the tremendous effort it takes to produce great food, will undoubtedly make a huge impact on the way any young cook views their profession."

THE FARMER

Roger Borrett, Kelowna

Roger Borrett grew up on an orchard in East Kelowna's orchard district. His current move into growing berries was driven from the basic fact that farming just apples would not pay the bills. Roger has been building relationships with chefs quickly with an impressive product to share - sweet berries.

In his own words:

"I grew up farming. My Grandfather bought the property in 1929 with my parents doing so in 1969. I left the farm in 1980 to pursue a career in engineering. In 1986 I returned home to help on the farm and ended up purchasing it in 1990. I started out only growing apples but have since planted berries, wine grapes, table grapes and some ground crops to obtain enough cash flow to survive.

I started to change my planting due to the fact that the apple industry was unable to return enough cash flow on a regular or even consistent basis. The main change I have seen in the last 20 years is the cost of operating and the lack of return from the market for our lower grade apples.

If I could grow all my apples in three sizes per variety, I would be able to do well but after all the overhead charges from the packing house in the last few years - if you break even, you are lucky.

A friend of mine got me into berries, ground crop and grapes through a friend's connection in the food industry. I find it very encouraging that local chefs seek out local products whenever they can and will pay a fair market value for them with many comments of appreciation and a sense of loyalty. These extra crops are a lot more work - but to get a fair return, it's worth the effort."

THE WINEMAKER

CedarCreek Estate Winery, Kelowna

Family owned CedarCreek Estate Winery has always been famous for its highly aromatic white wines and its smooth, fruit forward easy drinking reds. Owned by the Fitzpatrick family, the winery was originally Uniacke Winery, one of the first eight wineries in BC. Uniacke opened in 1980 and was sold to the Fitzpatricks in 1986. Senator Ross Fitzpatrick owns the winery with son Gordon operating it.

Winemaker Darryl Brooker is a graduate of Charles Sturt University in Australia (Bachelor of Applied Science - Wine Science) and also has a graduate diploma from Adelaide University in Wine Business.

The Terrace Restaurant patio is a gorgeous venue to enjoy Okanagan Lake and the surrounding vineyards. The restaurant has had a reputable line-up of chefs in the past including Chef Geoffrey Couper and Chef Judith Knight - Chef Robert Erickson is currently at the helm.

PAIRING

2011 CedarCreek Estate Winery Ehrenfelser

Made from 25-year-old vines, some call this wine "fruit salad in a glass" - and for good reason. Exploding with Okanagan stone fruits featuring nectarines this fresh tasting wine pairs well with summer and obviously is the perfect wine to make Geoffrey's Trembling Jelly.

WILD FLOWER HONEY-SAGE SEMIFREDDO, ROSE POACHED RHUBARB

PASTRY CHEF: ROBYN SIGURDSON, WILD APPLE RESTAURANT, KELOWNA
FARMER: BONNIE CASAVANT, EVERYTHING GREEN LANDSCAPING, WEST KELOWNA
WINEMAKER: TANTALUS VINEYARDS, KELOWNA

Semifreddo is another delicious creation from Italy. It's not ice cream, not gelato; its name means "half cold," referring to its texture. Okanagan rhubarb and Tantalus Riesling wine make this beautiful dish definitely Okanagan style. The hint of sage in the Semifreddo gives it a wonderful earthiness.

Serves 4

Wild Flower Honey- Sage Semifreddo:
6 egg yolks
4 tbsp Okanagan wild flower honey
orange, zest from 1/2 an orange (optional)
2 cups whipped cream
5 sage leaves

Using a loaf pan, line the inside of the pan with parchment paper, or plastic wrap. You can use any shape mold you wish; just make sure it is lined so it is easy to remove when frozen.
Place the sage in the cream for 2-3 hours to allow the flavour to infuse. Then remove the sage leaves and whip cream to medium peaks. Place in fridge.
Over a pot of simmering water in a stainless steel bowl, whisk the egg yolks and honey. Continue to whisk until the yolk mixture has thickened to about double the volume (Sabayon style). It will take a little while but continue to whisk the egg mixture until it thickens and when you lift the whisk and the egg mixture resembles a ribbon consistency.
At that point remove it from the heat, add a quarter of your whipping cream to the egg mixture gentling folding them together; do not deflate the whip cream. Once it has come together, then fold the egg mixture into the remaining whipped cream; again be cautious to fold gently with your spatula. When completely mixed together, pour into lined mold and freeze. Allow to freeze at least overnight before serving.

Tantalus Riesling Poached Rhubarb:
4 cups Okanagan rhubarb, washed, trimmed & diced
2 1/2 cups Tantalus Riesling
6 tbsp wild flower honey
optional garnish: fresh culinary flower and/or mint leaves

Combine the wine and honey - bring it to a simmer. Allow the rhubarb to poach until tender, and then remove. Reserve the wine liquid for plating your Okanagan summer dessert.

Assembly:
Place the poached rhubarb in the middle of a soup bowl; remove the Semifreddo from the freezer; invert on to a cutting board. Slice with a hot knife, or just scoop it out and place over poached fruit. Then pour your Tantalus Riesling poaching liquid around the bottom of the bowl. Garnish with culinary flowers and or mint leaves.

THE PASTRY CHEF

Robyn Sigurdson, Wild Apple Restaurant, Manteo Resort, Kelowna

Robyn has worked with some of the Okanagan's finest chefs. Her resume and talent led her to win the Okanagan Chef's Association Farm to Fork competition in 2010 that sent her to Italy to work on an agritourismo for three months.

In her own words:
"Born and raised in the Okanagan, my career path took a huge unexpected turn when I was in Grade 12 rather than going to a nursing program, I decided I loved my part time 6am baking shifts at Tim Horton's and so off I went to the Okanagan College Culinary Program. After a year in classroom and kitchen I started cooking at Summerhill Winery, where I was introduced to my first taste of organic food. From there I took a huge leap in my apprenticeship and traveled to Burrowing Owl Estate Winery where I worked for Chef Bernard Casavant and completed my apprentice training and received my Red Seal. I believe my time there instilled the cornerstones of what I represent when I put on my chef jacket today.

When you have the opportunity to walk the property of a farmer's land, it changes your perspective of those carrots, beets, apricots that come in the back door. It humbles you as a cook to have the opportunity to be able to create something beautiful on the plate. The relationship between restaurants and their suppliers is so important for the continued growth of the Farm to Plate way of cooking. It is critical because that relationship allows the kitchen to receive amazing local product that we take such pride to put on a plate; it also allows the supplier to have their business prosper and in some cases continue a legacy of farming that has continued for decades."

THE FARMER

Bonnie Casavant, Everything Green Landscaping, West Kelowna

Bonnie Casavant is a gardener and landscaper, and she is also the wife of our esteemed local Chef Bernard Casavant.

In her own words:
"I've always gardened, but it kicked into high gear when we moved to Kelowna. I took the Horticulture, Landscape Design, and Xeriscape courses at Okanagan College in 2007 and loved it so much I started my own landscape company! I love being outside; there is something Zen-like about digging in the dirt listening to the birds sing and all the summer noises on the lake. It's way more fun than accounting.

I started expanding my business this year and currently Manteo is my only customer. Ideally I'd like to sell to other restaurants but being my first year I'm still pretty small. I supply them with various vegetables, fruit, and herbs and also planted their herb garden and patio pots with tomatoes, herbs and edible flowers. The chefs are out on the patio pretty much every day cutting flowers and herbs to use in the kitchen.

It's nice to be involved with Chef Casavant again - I don't see the restaurant/kitchen side of things anymore since we left Burrowing Owl Winery. I work with him on what he would like me to plant; most products are on a trial basis and it has changed for next year already. I have been dabbling in growing micro greens as they use a ton of these in the restaurant - they are proving to be very finicky! An added bonus to supplying Manteo is that Chef takes the order in with him and I don't need to deliver weekly!"

THE WINEMAKER

David Paterson, Tantalus Vineyards, Kelowna

For many, Tantalus has become the benchmark for fine Rieslings. The vineyard is set on a historic, and incredibly scenic site in South East Kelowna and is managed by a team of passionate individuals. Senior winemaking consultant Jacqueline Kemp from New Zealand's Central Otago region works in tandem with Winemaker (another Kiwi) David Paterson – the two have created distinctive wines from the land's unique terroir. Tantalus Riesling is produced from 1985 and 2005 plantings of Mosel and Alsace clones, from 6 topographically different blocks in the 63-acre vineyard.

Not only known for their Riesling, Tantalus produces a Chardonnay, Dry Rosé, Pinot Noir, Riesling and Syrah Icewine with an Old Vines Riesling Sparkling wine new to their repertoire.

In his own words:
"I do not fine my wines so I leave phenolics in the wines to give balance and structure. They are high acid wines that help stimulate the taste buds and pair very well with food. I definitely take this into consideration when I make wine. I come from a restaurant background so I am always trying to create wines that pair with food."

PAIRING

2011 Tantalus Riesling

Pure aromatics of fresh guava, lime leaf and grapefruit zest, with subtle hints of wet stone and mineral. The palate is rich and inviting with flavours of candied lemon, juicy pear and granny smith apple. A refreshing line of natural acidity pulls the wine through to its laser focused, clean finish."

Okanagan Cheese Board

1. Happy Days Goat Cheese: Fresh Goat Cheese in Herb Oil
2. Carmelis Goat Cheese Artisan - Chevry Dill & Onion
3. Upper Bench Creamery - Grey Baby
4. Upper Bench Okanagan Sun2
5. Triple Island Gouda - Mild
6. Poplar Grove Cheese - Camembert
7. Poplar Grove Cheese - Naramata Bench Blue

Cheese board is made by Broken Barrel Furniture Co., Penticton and is made from a used wine barrel top (underneath is red wine stained).

Spelt Hazelnut Raisin Crackers

Chef: Mary de Bakker, De Bakker's Kitchen, Kelowna
Farmer: Urs Baumann, Quail's Farm, Vernon
Winemakers: Little Farm Winery, Cawston/Black Hills Winery, Oliver/ Squeezed Wines, Oliver

These crackers are completely whole grain, wheat free, refined sugar free, vegan, and addictive. Mary uses a lot of local ingredients in them. Their spelt comes from Urs' Quail's Farm in Vernon. The poppy seeds are collected by Mary's children from their garden. Local raisins, walnuts and hazelnuts can also be used when available.

This recipe was tested using a convection oven. Baking temperature should be increased by 25 º F for baking in a conventional oven.

1/4 cup flax seed
1/2 cup hazelnuts
1 teaspoon loose leaf organic Earl Grey tea
1/2 cup maple syrup
1 1/2 teaspoons fine sea salt
3 1/2 cups whole grain spelt flour
2 tbps + 2 tsp baking powder
2 cups organic raisins
3/4 cup walnuts, coarsely chopped
1/4 cup poppy seeds
1 cup hazelnuts

Position top oven rack in the center of your oven. Preheat oven to 300ºF. Toast 1 1/2 cups hazelnuts on a sheet pan for approximately 5 minutes. Remove nuts from the oven and rub warm nuts with a clean cotton dish towel to remove as much skin as possible. Put 1/2 cup of hazelnuts in blender and add 1 cup water. Blend on high for approximately 3 minutes. Line a fine mesh strainer with cheese cloth and strain. You should have about 1 cup of hazelnut milk. If you have less, top up with water to make 1 cup. Reserve ground hazelnuts for another use or discard. Coarsely chop the other 1 cup of hazelnuts and set aside.

Add 1/2 teaspoon of loose leaf Earl Grey tea to ½ cup boiling water. Let steep 5 minutes and strain.

Make flax purée. Put 1/4 cup flax seed in a blender and turn on high to grind. Slowly pour in ¾ cup of water and let blender run for about 3 minutes. Measure out 1/4 of this purée and refrigerate the rest for another use.

In a large bowl whisk together 3 ½ cups whole grain spelt flour with 2 tablespoons + 2 teaspoons baking powder.

In another bowl whisk together ¼ cup flax purée, 1 cup hazelnut milk, 1/2 cup brewed Earl Grey tea, 1/2 cup maple syrup, 1 1/2 teaspoons fine sea salt.

In a third bowl combine 2 cups raisins, 3/4 chopped walnuts, 1/4 cup poppy seeds, and the reserved 1 cup of toasted and chopped hazelnuts.

Prepare 2 loaf pans (approximately 9" x 5" size). Brush with vegetable oil and line with parchment paper to prevent sticking.

Pour wet ingredients into dry ingredients and fold until flour is moistened. Fold in raisin- nut mixture. Divide dough between the two loaf pans and bake for about 1 hour or until a toothpick inserted in the center of the loaf comes out clean. Remove loaves from the pans and let cool on a wire rack. When they are room temperature, wrap in plastic and refrigerate for at least 8 hours and up to a day.

Preheat oven to 250ºF. Using a serrated knife slice loaves into pieces about 1/8" thick. Lay slices out on a parchment lined sheet pan and bake for approximately 45 minutes rotating trays after 25 minutes if you have several racks of crackers baking at once. You will probably have to bake these in batches. One batch fits perfectly in a commercial convection oven. Remove sheet pans from the oven and flip crackers over. When they are completely dried and cooled, store in an airtight container. This recipe makes a lot of crackers but they keep well and make great gifts.

THE CHEF

Mary De Bakker, De Bakker's Kitchen, Kelowna

Mary De Bakker and her husband Sandy Lukic own and operate De Bakker's Kitchen – a bakery/ restaurant specializing in wood-fire oven pizza. Located in Kelowna's Glemore neighbourhood, Sandy and Mary are serious locavores and are huge supporters of our local farmers. Focusing on the old world sustainability model, the two chose to use local apple wood for their oven. They also use local flour, supplied by Urs Baumann's Certified Organic Quail's Farm in Vernon. Sandy says, "I love the old world feeling of having Urs deliver his farm milled flour to the restaurant - this renaissance signals the direction of the future."

Mary DeBakker (R)
and Sandy Lukic

THE FARMER

Urs Baumann, Quail's Farm, Vernon

Urs owns and operates a small organic farm located in Vernon BC. The farm offers fresh milled organic spelt flour, baked goods, eggs and produce. Products are available at the Vernon Farmers' Market and the Kelowna Farmers' Market. Also available at Anna's Vitamins in Vernon & Nature's Fare.

A baker by trade, Urs moved here from Switzerland in 1993 and after planting a garden he says, "I realized that I liked farming more than baking!"

Urs met Sandy and Mary at the Kelowna Farmers' Market when they too were vendors and they have continued the relationship ever since.

WINEMAKERS

Little Farm Wines, Cawston

Our local celebrated Master of Wine Rhys Pender's long anticipated first vintage of wine was released this year in October, 2012. Under the label Little Farm, named for he and his wife Alishan's beautiful old farmhouse in the Similkameen, they have released two wines: a Chardonnay and a Riesling.

PAIRING:
2012 Little Farm Riesling
Riesling is a great wine to pair with cheeses.
This version is a pure expression of the vineyard showcasing the minerality derived from the calcium carbonate soil. Aromas of apple, chalk, honeydew melon, lemon and lime zest lead on to an unashamedly dry and steely palate with lime juice-like intensity and lots of powerful mineral flavours. The acidity is high and crisp and racy, with the lime and lemon flavours followed by complex mandarin, stone fruit, honeydew melon and chalk with great length.
Try this wine with Triple Island Gouda or goat cheese.

Black Hills Winery, Oliver

This renowned winery maintains a celebrity status in the wine world – not only because of one of its celebrity shareholders – but because of its wine celebrity aka Note Bene.

This rich and dynamic red wins over palates of every level and has achieved a cult following over the past few years. Winemaker Graham Pierce, has a large repertoire of both reds and whites on offer and the actual winery in Oliver has recently renovated adding a new wine tasting experience. Guests will attend mini seminars on wine tasting in house conducted by their "wine evangelists".

PAIRING: **2010 Black Hills Estate Winery Note Bene**
A Bordeaux-style red blend, that since its first release in 1999, continues to thrill. A blend of 57% Cabernet Sauvignon • 32% Merlot • 11% Cabernet Franc. "Aromas of chocolate, star anise, spicy pepper, raspberry and cloves come forth on the nose. On the palate there is great weight and nice tannin intensity. This gives way to flavours of mocha, cherry cola, coffee and chocolate with a subtle hint of smoky leather and cigar box."
Try this cheese with the Poplar Grove Camembert Cheese or Upper Bench's Okanagan Gold.

Michael & Christina Ferreira

Squeezed Wines, Oliver

Born and raised in Oliver, BC, Christina, Nicole and Michael Ferreira grew up on an orchard, spending their summers picking and packaging all soft fruits in their parents packinghouse. Coming from an agricultural family, the trio learned hard work ethics at early ages. Their desire to explore an exciting adventure, staying true to their agricultural roots alongside 10 years experience in the wine industry got their brains thinking how to take their passion and create a vision. With farming in their blood and wine in their hearts, starting a winery sounded like the perfect venture for the siblings to undertake. And so Squeezed was born.

PAIRING:
Squeezed White – A blend of Sauvignon Blanc, Chardonnay and Viognier. Squeezed White is off-dry and pairs with mild to medium aged cheeses and soft cheeses.

HOMEMADE

Emma Mae's Chocolate Chip Zucchini Loaf

Debbie Donahue, Tasty Treasures, Kelowna

Debbie Donahue just opened her own shop in Orchard Park Mall, Tasty Treasures, featuring her delicious baked goods after being a regular at the Kelowna Farmers' Market. Originally from Grindrod, Debbie said that she remembers baking this zucchini loaf with her Grandma, Emma Mae Wright – it was a favorite and is a wonderful example of utilizing garden vegetables in baking.

Ingredients:
1/4 cup butter
1 3/4 cup sugar
1/2 cup oil
2 eggs
1 tsp vanilla
1/2 cup buttermilk
2 1/2 cup flour
1/4 cup cocoa
1/2 tsp baking powder
1 tsp baking soda
1/2 tsp cinnamon
1/2 tsp ground cloves
2 cup zucchini, grated
2/3 cup chocolate chips

Cream butter and sugar. Add eggs and beat until light and fluffy. Slowly pour in oil and mix until combined. Add vanilla and buttermilk and mix until combined. Sift all dry ingredients together and add to creamed mixture and blend until the flour is well incorporated. Fold in zucchini and chocolate chips. Pour into two 5x9 lightly greased loaf pans or one lightly greased bundt pan. Bake in a preheated 350°F oven for 55-60 minutes.

FRESH PEACH PIE

JENNIFER SCHELL

This particular recipe is so delicious because it highlights the true flavour of the peach. Easy as um... er pie, fresh sliced peaches are added to a cooked pie shell and topped with whipped cream - the results are just peachy!

Crust:
1/1/4 cups all-purpose flour
1 1/2 tsp. baking powder
1/2 tsp salt
6 ounces cream cheese, room temperature
6 tbsp unsalted butter, softened
1 1/2 tsp pure vanilla extract
1/4 cup sugar

Filling:
8 - 9 ripe peaches, peeled and sliced
1/2 cup sugar
1 cup whipping cream

Make crust: Sift flour, baking powder and salt into bowl – mix well. In an electric mixer beat cream cheese and butter to blend. Add vanilla and stir then add sugar and stir to blend. Add flour mixture and mix thoroughly – do not over mix. Flour hands and form dough into flat round, wrap in plastic wrap and refrigerate for an hour. Lightly flour work surface and roll out dough into a 12-inch round at 1/4 to 1/2 inch thick. Press dough lightly into pie plate, trim excess dough and fork edges. Cover with plastic wrap and refrigerate from 30 minutes or overnight. Bake crust at 350°F for 30 minutes or until golden and puffy then remove and cool completely.
For filling: Mix sliced peaches with 1/4 cup sugar and pour over crust. Whip cream until soft peaks form, then add remaining 1/4 cup sugar and beat until stiff. Cover peaches with whipped cream and refrigerate for a minimum of 2 hours maximum of 8 hours – Enjoy!
(Note: increase sugar measure if peaches are not sweet.)

GRANDMA'S RELISH

KATE WEISBECK

This tangy and sweet relish is so easy to make these days with food processors doing all the chopping for us. A definite family favorite, this recipe hails from my Grandma Kate Weisbeck's large repertoire of delicious canned and baked goods. This recipe also represents a celebration of the bounty found in an Okanagan summer garden. (P.S. Grandma is 95 years old now – maybe this relish is the secret!)

8 large cucumbers, peeled
4 cups onions
4 cups celery
2 green peppers
2 red peppers
1/2 cup salt

Whizz in food processor until finely chopped – then let sit for a minimum 2 hours – maximum overnight. Drain, rinse and then drain well again.

Add:
4 cups white vinegar
6 cups white sugar
1/2 cup flour
3/4 cup cold white vinegar
1 tbsp turmeric
4 tbsp mustard
1 tbsp celery seed
1 tsp mustard seed

Bring sugar and vinegar to boil. Mix dry ingredients with cold vinegar. Add hot mixture of sugar and vinegar and then cook until it thickens (about 20-25 minutes or until thickness suits you). Add vegetables and boil hard for 10 minutes. Pour into sterilized heated jars and seal with sterilized lids.

Mom's Rhubarb Pie

Marion Schell

This easy pie is absolutely scrumptious and is a unique addition to your regular fruit pie favourites. The brilliant ruby red colour of rhubarb makes this the perfect springtime dessert to celebrate the first growth in your garden.

4 cups rhubarb
1 tsp baking soda
2 eggs
1 tbsp milk
1 1/2 cups sugar
1/3 cup flour
1 tbsp butter, room temperature
1 unbaked pie shell (pie can be made without a top pastry layer or with lattice as shown in photo)

Pour hot water over rhubarb in a large bowl, stir in baking soda and let sit.
In mixer, beat together eggs, milk, flour, sugar and butter.
Drain rhubarb and add to mixer.
Fill unbaked pie shell (arrange lattice topping if using.)
Bake for 1 1/2 hours at 350°F on oven rack (one below middle.)
Let cool and enjoy!

Dale Ziech and
Donna Denison

MRS. SMITH'S PRUNE PLUM CHUTNEY

DONNA DENISON, LITTLE CREEK GARDENS, WEST KELOWNA

Mr. Smith stayed with my Grandparents in their small log home in Creighton Valley (near Lumby, BC). He shared this recipe with my Nana.

12 cups prune plums
4 cups apples
3 large onions
3 ½ -4 cups brown sugar
½ tsp ginger
1 ½ tsp cinnamon
2 tsp cloves
2 cups vinegar (or 1 cup white vinegar plus
¾ cup apple cider)
salt to taste
½ orange put through food chopper
juice of ½ lemon

Peel and grate apples, grate onions, put through food chopper with orange. Pit prune plums
Combine and simmer for 2 hours. Makes 11- 250 ml jars + 1- 125 ml jar

Donna Denison and husband Dale Ziech became local celebrities after introducing their organic Little Creek Salad Dressings and Greens to the food industry.

In her own words:
"Celebrations have to be made...troubles come on their own." The incredible beauty and energy that comes from a tiny seed inspires me...also there is something very healing and uplifting about plants that touches me deeply. Sometimes in the most adverse situations, plants live and survive; it is a lesson for us all to persevere and keep growing! For Dale, he had a realization that along with air and water, food gives us life, and he wanted to be sure to know how to grow his own food so he could feed himself and others."

On family history:
"On both sides of my family, there were gardeners. My maternal Grandmother lived for her garden, for growing things and gathering wild plants for teas and healing. Mother always planted a large vegetable garden and I remember her planting her flower garden and trees at our new house in the 60's even before we moved in. We spent our summers in the Okanagan and Mom would always can fruit, make jam, bake bread, make soups and put out food for not only our family, but for many of our friends. On my Father's side, there were gardeners as well.

My Grandfather, Norman Denison, was known as the "Turnip King" and my Nana would always say she never thought she would marry a farmer, but she did!
My Nana, Ethel Gibbs, was born in Enderby. Her Grandfather was a private messenger to Queen Victoria, and I guess her parents decided to set off for the adventure of coming to Canada, specifically the Okanagan.
On my Granddad's side: the Denison family was asked to help settle the new lands and were amongst the original settlers in Toronto (specifically, York, which is the name Captain John Denison told Simcoe he wanted to name the new settlement). In later years some of the sons moved west to settle and my Grandfather was born in Calgary. His family came by covered wagon (or Red River carts) to settle in the Okanagan when he was just a baby. His parents settled in the Coldstream area and socialized with Lord and Lady Aberdeen who owned the Coldstream Ranch in those days.
My dreams (for the future) would be that farmers would be honoured, respected and acknowledged more and that they would be able to make a decent living growing food. As well it would be wonderful to have more small artisan producers which I feel is happening - it would also be amazing to have the valley totally organic and keep it GMO free!"

OMA'S PRUNE KUCHEN

JULIANNA SCHELL

This kuchen is my Oma, Julianna Schell's recipe and it rates a close second in the Schell family favorites recipe file (first will always be apple pie). I love the versatility and the size of this coffee cake cooked on a baking sheet. The trick of using vanilla sugar was a recent alteration to the recipe by my Mom, Marion Schell (pictured left).

Topping:
1 cup flour
1/2 cup sugar
1 pkg vanilla sugar (local suggestion:
Illichmanns Meats, Sausages & Gourmet Foods)
1/2 cup cold butter

Batter:
2 cups flour
3 tsp baking powder
1 tsp salt
1 cup sugar
2 eggs
2/3 cup vegetable oil
1 cup milk
2 tsp vanilla
1/2 tsp lemon juice
12 local Italian prune plums (long purple oval
shaped), washed, dried, quartered and pitted
(or enough to make one layer on batter)
10x15 high rimmed baking sheet

Preheat oven to 350°F. Make topping by combining all dry ingredients and cutting in the cold butter with a pastry cutter until a coarse meal texture is achieved (you can also use your food processor to achieve this by pulsating the chop button).

For batter, combine dry ingredients in a large bowl. Mix wet ingredients in another smaller bowl. Add wet ingredients to dry ingredients using wooden spoon and mix well. Pour into pan. Spread fruit over batter in a generous layer. Top with crumb mixture. Bake approximately 35-40 minutes until lightly browned. Refrigerate leftovers. Freezes well. This cake works well with other Okanagan fruits or berries like apricots, apples, cherries or blueberries, so you can vary your cake by the season.

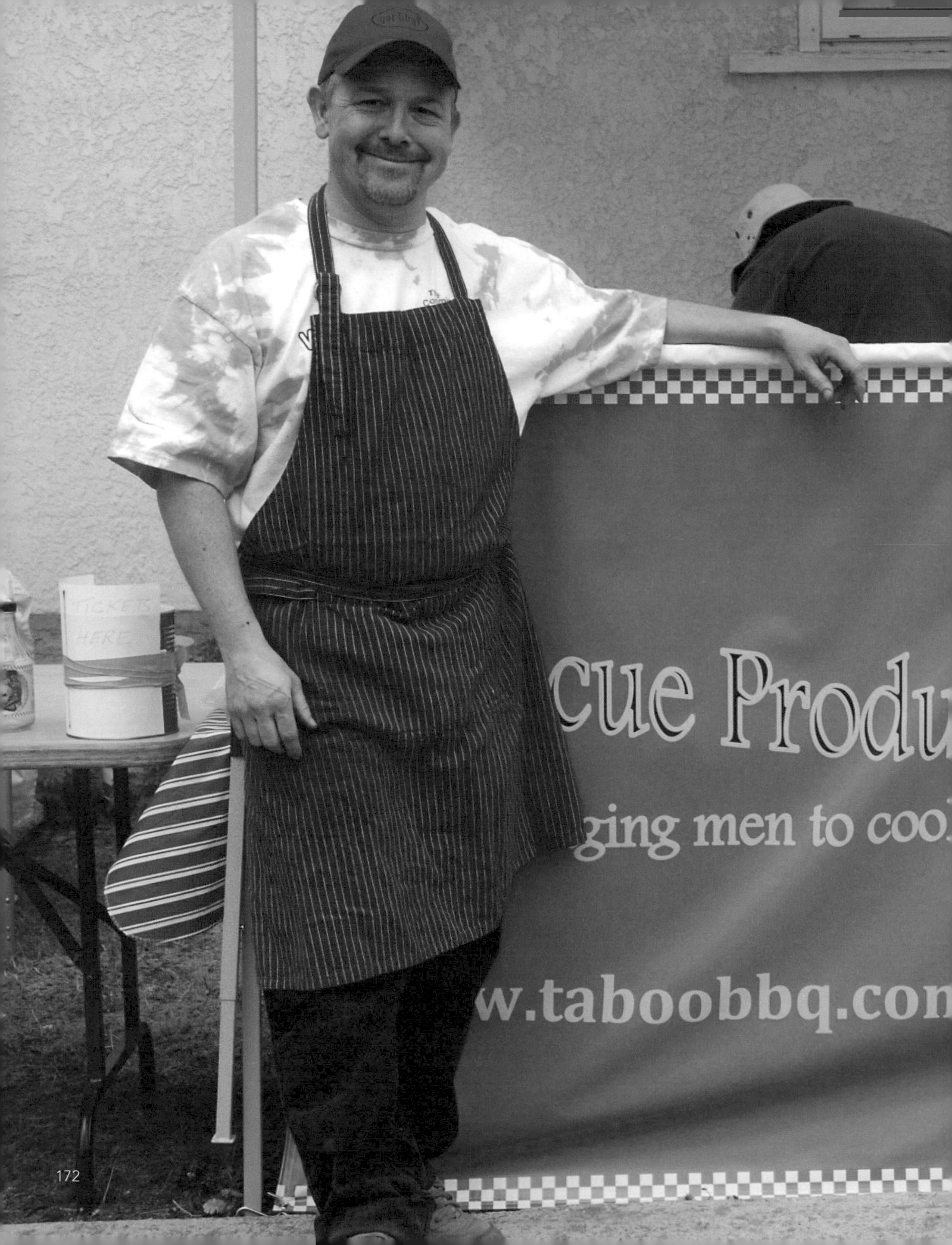
TICKETS HERE
cue Produ
ging men to coo
w.taboobbq.con

ORCHARDIST FRUIT BBQ SAUCE

CHEF MARTIN LAPRISE

Chef Martin Laprise aka The Chef Instead is involved in a wide range of food activities in the Okanagan. He caters, he makes a line of BBQ spice rubs, he educates and he enjoys the very best of the Okanagan from his headquarters, Rabbit Hollow in West Kelowna.
His recent project has been transforming his own backyard into an agritourism destination to host dinners and events.

Ingredients:

A)
1/2 red onion, chopped
1/2 sweet red pepper, chopped
1 tbsp fresh ginger, chopped fine or grated
1 fresh garlic clove, minced

B)
3/4 cup apple cider vinegar
1/2 cup brown sugar
1/2 cup white sugar
4 tbsp honey
1/4 cup Worcestershire sauce

C)
3 cups pitted fresh cherries
1 tbsp dried New Mexican chile pepper, ground
(substitute crushed red chili flakes
if you can't find this kind of chile)
1 tsp dried ancho pepper, ground
1/2 tsp dried chipotle pepper, ground
1 tbsp dark chili powder
1 tbsp smoked paprika
2 tsp garlic powder
2 tsp ginger powder
1/4 tsp cinnamon
3/4 tsp cloves
1/2 tsp ground cumin
2 sprigs fresh thyme
2 sprigs fresh rosemary
5 drops liquid smoke (optional)

Sweat A ingredients with a touch of olive oil in a heavy-duty, non-reactive saucepan. Add B ingredients to pan and bring to a boil. Add C ingredients and simmer for about 30 minutes or until desired thickness is reached, stirring occasionally so that it does not stick to the bottom.
You can leave the sauce more "rustic" or blend it for a smoother consistency. Sauce will keep refrigerated for up to 7-10 days (but it's so good it probably won't last that long). Chef Martin likes this sauce with cherries served over pork ribs, tenderloin or chops but it works well with apricots or peaches over chicken and plums will work too. (Same quantity of fruit, everything else stays the same.) Of course, you can choose your favourite Okanagan wine to match!

In his own words:
"Everything at Rabbit Hollow is visual as much as tasty. We want to show people a good time and make sure that when they leave they remember this experience for the rest of their lives for the quality of food but mostly for how much fun they had with us."

PENNY'S FAVOURITE SASKATOON PIE

PENNY GAMBELL

Penny Gambell of Gambell Farms in Lake Country explains, "We planted our Smokey Saskatoons in a small orchard below our house, 21 years ago. These bushes grew from seed brought in from Beaverlodge, Alberta, so they have small seeds, lots of juice, and are much sweeter than the wild berries in our Okanagan hills." Such a unique flavour. Make sure to visit Gambell Farms at the farmers' market in Kelowna or at their farm stand at home in Lake Country to pick up these berries next spring. They make a delicious jam too!

4 cups Smokey Saskatoons
3/4 cup sugar
2 tsp lemon juice
water
2 to 3 tablespoons cornstarch

Cover the Saskatoons with water and simmer on low heat for about 20 minutes. Add sugar, lemon juice and stir to dissolve. Keep out about 1/2 cup of water to dissolve the cornstarch. Add cornstarch to Saskatoon mixture, and stir to ensure it is well blended, and no lumps form. Simmer on low to cook the mixture about 5 minutes longer or until thickened and clear. You may add more or less cornstarch depending on how thick you want the pie filling. When cooled, add to pastry-lined dish, cover with pastry, and bake in convection oven at 400°F for approximately 25 minutes or until pastry is golden around the edges.

Variation: Saskatoon-Rhubarb pie
This is essentially the same recipe, but you need to add 1 cup of chopped rhubarb to the Saskatoons as you are boiling them at the start. You may want to increase the sugar to 1 cup or more to taste, and you will not need the lemon juice.
Penny says that both recipes yield an excellent sauce for pancakes or on ice cream. They can also be used in a crisp.

ZWIEBELKUCHEN (ONION QUICHE)

STEFANIE SCHALES

8th Generation Vineyard in Summerland is known for its delicious, crisp German-style wines including the addition of two Frizzantes. Winemaking has been a continuous tradition in their family for well over 225 years. Bernd Schales is an 8th generation Winemaker and his wife, Stefanie is a 10th generation grapegrower – together they have created a new tradition for their children here in Canada. This recipe is a family tradition and marks the harvest time celebrating the first crush, served with glasses of Neuer wine – the still fermenting white wine. (The wine has to be still sweet, cloudy and bubbly). Note: ask your local winery friends if you can buy a jug – I know Stefanie and Bernd would be happy to sell you some.

Dough:
2 cups flour
4 tsp yeast
¼ cup butter
1 egg
½ cup milk
½ tsp salt

First rise: Mix the yeast with some of the warm milk, add a pinch of sugar and let it sit on a warm spot to rise.

Second rise: Put the flour in a large mixing bowl, add the egg, butter, salt and the rest of the milk and work with the dough hooks, then add the warm yeast mixture.

Knead for at least 5 minutes until it is one dough ball. Add additional milk or flour if the dough is to dry or wet.

Cover the dough with a clean tea towel and let it sit on a warm spot until it's doubled in size.

Filling:
1 kg (or 5 large) sweet onions fine chopped
3 slices Schinkenspeck (local suggestion: Illichmann's Deli) or good bacon, finely chopped
2 eggs
1 tablespoon flour
1 cup sour cream
½ tsp salt
½ tsp caraway seeds

Sauté the finely chopped onions in a large pot on low for 20 minutes until soft then add the finely chopped Schinkenspeck or bacon (do not brown the onions). Remove from heat and let the onions chill down and enjoy a glass of wine- nearly done! Sprinkle the flour on top of the onions, add the eggs, sour cream, caraway seeds and salt and blend together with a wooden spoon.

Put the dough on a sprinkled flour surface (countertop), and roll it to the size of your baking tray (traditionally it is baked on a round pizza pan - diameter ~ 38cm). Grease your pan. Create a 2cm high "curb" on the rim of the tray. Fill the (unbaked) dough with the topping and bake it at 350 degrees for 45 minutes, until it is nicely browned.

Okanagan Festivals & Events

GRINDROD GARLIC FESTIVAL

The 3rd Annual Garlic Festival in beautiful Grindrod happens in August. Hosted by the Grindrod Recreation Association at the Grindrod Park there is a flurry of activities celebrating local garlic and produce. Grindrod is absolutely stunning and full of beautiful farms – it is the perfect place to celebrate this beloved stinky bulb.

If anyone knows how to cook a chicken properly it is a farmer. Here Gabriele Wesle from Green Croft Gardens in Grindrod shares a delicious recipe that is a true celebration of garlic. Gabriele and husband Wolf are very involved in the Annual Garlic Festival in Grindrod. Son Simon won the raw garlic eating contest in 2012!

CHICKEN WITH 40 CLOVES OF GARLIC

2 celery stalks
2 rosemary sprigs
4 thyme sprigs
1-4 lb chicken
40 garlic cloves, unpeeled
2 tbsp olive oil
1 carrot , chopped coarsely
1 small onion, quartered
1 cup Okanagan white wine
1 baguette, sliced

Preheat oven to 400°F. Put a chopped celery stalk and 2 sprigs each of the rosemary, thyme and parsley into the chicken cavity. Add 10 cloves of garlic. Tie the legs together and tuck the wingtips under. Brush the chicken liberally with the oil and season well. Arrange about 10 more garlic cloves over the bottom of a large casserole. Put the remaining sprigs of herbs, chopped celery, carrot and onion in the casserole.
Put the chicken in the casserole. Scatter the remaining garlic cloves and the remaining oil and wine around the chicken. Cover and bake for about 80-90 minutes or until the chicken is done and juices run clear when the thigh is pierced.
Carefully remove the chicken from the casserole. Strain off the juices into a small sauce pan. Use tongs to pick out the garlic cloves from the strained mixture. Spoon off any fat from the juices and boil for 3-4 minutes to thicken a little.
Cut the chicken into portions, pour over the juices and scatter with the garlic. Toast the baguette slices, then garnish the chicken with sprigs of herbs and serve the bread to be spread with the soft flesh squeezed from the garlic.

Gabriele Wesle

181

FARM FOLK
CITY FOLK

METRO VANCOUVER · OKANAGAN · VANCOUVER ISL

OKANAGAN FEAST OF FIELDS

FarmFolk/CityFolk organizes three Annual Feast of Fields events during August and September, one in the Lower Mainland, one on Vancouver Island, and the Okanagan. Basically, the theme of the event is a four hour wandering harvest festival, a celebration of the local harvest and provides an opportunity for city folks to spend an afternoon at a farm, sampling the best of BC's local food and beverages. Feast of Fields also provides a networking opportunity for farmers and chefs, vintners and brewers, food service professionals and artisan food producers. Feast of Fields is also a wonderful opportunity for small-scale producers to introduce new product lines to potential buyers. Like this cookbook, Feast of Fields highlights "the connections between farmer and chef, field and table, and farm folks and city folks. Feast of Fields is also described as a gastronomic journey towards a sustainable, local food system." The Okanagan just celebrated their 4th year of hosting a Feast at Claremont Ranch Organics in Lake Country. The event moves to different locations throughout the valley each year. www.feastoffields.com

KILLER TOMATO COCKTAIL

Raudz Liquid Chef Gerry Jobe took the humble tomato and gave a new twist to the Bloody Mary – "The Killer Tomato" demonstrating that even behind the bar... fresh & local can also go into a cocktail shaker.

1oz vodka
1oz cointreau
0.25 ounce balsamico
4 muddled Sungold tomatoes
3 ounces of lemonade

Shaken over ice, double-strained into a coupe glass rimmed with crushed szechuan peppercorns and sel gris.

Cheers!

OKANAGAN WHITE DINNER

The inaugural Okanagan White Dinner was a huge success this year. The committee team (Alison Love, Christina Ferreira, Claire Sear, Jennifer Schell) had a true battle with the elements setting up that day, but in the end earth, wind nor fire could keep the spirit of this Parisian-style pop up picnic down.

High winds during set up not only caused our team headaches it was also the instigator of Peachland's disastrous fire, spreading it into dangerous rural territory. The first call was from friends, who needed to cancel in order to get home, pack and get their dogs to safety; the second was sadly from our shuttle driver bringing our white merrymakers to the party from down south. The

bus was stopped and turned around by police. The good news? This group's unstoppable spirit landed them at one of the shuttler's homes and they proceeded to pop up their own party in sync with ours via cyberspace. It was so heartwarming viewing the photos of the mini white party waving their napkins in their air – the traditional signal that the group approves of the secret location and to let the party begin.

The event sold out with 200 people attending this beautiful picnic and the Okanagan could not have looked more glamorous. Attendees were in full white – from white tuxes, to hats and fascinators, feathers and glitz together all toasting the night with glasses of bubble

on a backdrop of lake, mountains (and unfortunately fire red sky) – we were a Gatsby-esque delight. And, disappearing as quickly as the flash mob arrived – just as the original organizer François Pasquier over 20 years ago planned – it felt like a dream. We can't wait until next year.

We are in negotiations with the international committee from Le Diner en Blanc to make our Okanagan event an official part of their international organization. We will then hopefully become Diner En Blanc next year allowing the world to gaze upon our beautiful Valley and its fabulous inhabitants. Le yay! Check out their website for details on this event: www.dinerenblanc.info

185

PATÉ EN BLANC

BRENT BEASLEY

My friend Brent came up with this delicious Okanagan inspired paté to serve at the Diner en Blanc we attended in Vancouver.

Ingredients:

1/2 cup (1 stick) unsalted butter
1 pound fresh chicken livers, trimmed and patted dry
coarse salt and freshly ground black pepper
5 shallots, sliced
2 ripe Okanagan Bartlett pears, cored and chopped
3 large fresh thyme sprigs, plus more for garnish
3 whole cloves
2 sticks cinnamon
1 tablespoon light-brown sugar
1/4 cup pear brandy (local suggestion: Okanagan Spirits)
3 tablespoons heavy cream
2 tablespoons balsamic reduction (local suggestion: Nona Pia's Balsamic Reduction - they are in Whistler but still qualify as BC local)
3/4 teaspoon freshly grated nutmeg
clarified butter, melted
Maldon sea salt, for serving

Directions

Heat 2 tablespoons butter in a large high-sided skillet over medium-high heat. Season livers with salt and pepper; add to skillet and cook, turning once, until just cooked through (liver may be slightly pink inside), about 4 minutes per side. Remove livers from skillet and set aside.

Reduce heat to medium and add another tablespoon butter to skillet. Add shallots and season with salt and pepper; cook, stirring, until translucent, about 5 minutes. Add pears, thyme, cloves, cinnamon sticks, brown sugar, and 1/4 cup water. Cover and cook, stirring occasionally and adding water as necessary to prevent burning, until pears are soft and easily pierced with the tip of a sharp knife, about 15 minutes. Remove skillet from heat; uncover and add brandy, scraping up browned bits at bottom of skillet to deglaze. Remove thyme and cinnamon sticks from skillet and discard.

Cut remaining 5 tablespoons butter into small cubes. Transfer remaining contents of skillet to the bowl of a food processor along with chicken livers, cream, vinegar, nutmeg, and cut butter. Process until mixture is very smooth; season with salt and pepper.

Strain chicken liver mousse through a fine mesh sieve, using a spatula to push mousse through sieve. Transfer to jars and top each with a sprig of fresh thyme. Add enough clarified butter to top of chicken liver mousse to form a thin film, about 1/16 of an inch; cover and transfer to refrigerator to chill. Keep chilled until ready to serve, up to 1 week. Serve with sea salt, jam, and toasts.

Brent Beasley
en blanc

L-R: John & Virginia Weber (Orofino Vineyards), Dana Ewart and Cameron Smith (Joy Road Catering)

THE CHEFS

Cameron and Dana, Joy Road Catering, Penticton

Cameron and Dana of Joy Road Catering are the quintessential locavorian chefs. With a booming catering business taking them up and down the valley at some of the most anticipated events of the year, each dish is created with a true focus on local, seasonal produce and happy animals.

They also cater a regular al fresco dinner series up at God's Mountain Vineyard through the summer season. As business builds so does their own farm and gardens allowing them to basically shop at home and knowing exactly where and how their food was created and raised.

OROFINO WINERY'S 1.6 MILE DINNER

THE CHEFS: CAMERON SMITH & DANA EWART, JOY ROAD CATERING, PENTICTON
THE HOSTS: JOHN & VIRGINIA WEBER, OROFINO VINEYARDS, CAWSTON
THE FARMERS: BLAIR AND CHERYL COREY, DAN THE MILK MAN,
ELAINE, FOREST, GABRIELLE, DAVE, JUSTENE, JOHN AND VIRGINIA LAUREN,
PAUL, LEAH, MOSESS, SHIRLEY MAE, PHILLIPA, ERIC, RENATE, PHYLIS
THE WINEMAKERS: OROFINO VINEYARDS, CAWSTON/SEVEN STONES WINERY, CAWSTON

STARTER:
"A STUDY IN YELLOW":
GOLDEN BEET & APRICOT SALAD WITH FRESH RICOTTA & FENNEL

Serves 6

1/2 pint golden raspberries
6 golden beets
3 ripe apricots
1 bulb fennel with fronds
2 tbsp cider vinegar
2 small shallots
salt (Maldon and kosher)
1/2 cup good olive oil
1 cup ricotta or other fresh cheese

Cook the beets in their skins in enough salted water to cover. They are done when easily pierced with a knife. Slip off the skins while they are still warm. When cool, slice the beets into 1/4 inch coins.

Viniagrette:
Finely dice the shallots and macerate them in the vinegar with a pinch of kosher salt. Slowly whisk in the olive oil, and season to taste.

Assembly:
Shave the fennel finely on a mandolin. Place in cool water to help it curl and remain crunchy. Pick off some nice fine fronds for garnish. (Tarragon leaves are also a lovely garnish for this salad.) Halve and pit the apricots.

To serve:
Arrange the sliced beets, apricot halves, shaved fennel and cheese on the plate.
Drizzle with the vinaigrette- stirring it well beforehand.
Season with Maldon salt and garnish with fronds.

Fresh Ricotta:
4L homogenized milk
500ml 35% cream
1L buttermilk

Heat all dairy in a heavy bottomed non reactive pot. Over medium heat, stirring every now and then so that it doesn't scorch on the bottom of the pot until it reaches 160°F, then leave it. Turn off the heat once it reaches 185°F allowing the curds to separate fully from the whey for about 1 hour to cool slowly.
Take a spoon with small holes in it to spoon the curds in to a strainer double lined with cheesecloth. Leave hanging in the fridge overnight to drain.

189

WINEMAKER:
George Hanson, Seven Stones Winery, Cawston

This beautiful winery overlooks a green valley in Cawston. George Hanson is known for his winemaking and for his unique soil that contains layers of sandy loam, limestone and clay. "Burgundy and Bordeaux right there! We are the only area that has this limestone layer in the soil," says George.

The Hansons' lovely home next door and wineshop design can be accredited to George's beautiful wife Vivianne who sadly passed away this summer. Her sparkling spirit can be felt at the winery and her memory will live on through the many who adored her in this close-knit community.

MAIN:
Poulet Persille, Chicken & Egg Conundrum: chicken terrine with Gabrielle's haricot vert, pickled pink shallots, tarragon bearnaise from Corey's eggs

PAIRING:
2009 Seven Stones Chardonnay

1- 5 lb chicken, de-boned (Joy Road prefers using the happy chickens from Richard at North Okanagan Game Meats)
1 terrine mould
1 bottle of Okanagan white wine (local suggestion: Seven Stones Chardonay.)

Brine:
4L water
200g sea salt
125g brown sugar
1 head of garlic, halved
10 peppercorns
2 bay leaves

Bring to the boil 1L of the water with all other ingredients. Add cold water to this mixture after all of the salt and sugar have dissolved. When cooled, add the de-boned chicken and allow to brine for 24 hours submerged in the brine in the fridge. Make a stock with the chicken bones using 1L of water plus 1 bottle of Okanagan white wine. Then take the skin off of the chicken, and poach the brined chicken meat until it is soft in the strained stock. Strain the stock again after the chicken is removed.

Terrine:
Ingredients:
1L of chicken stock
4 sheets gelatin
4.5 lbs chicken (poached in the stock, cooled, then pulled in to 1cm diameter strips)
2 bunches fresh flat leaf parsley from the garden, washed, dried, then chiffonade
1/8 cup shallot, finely diced
2 tbsp tarragon vinegar

Assembly:
Line a terrine mould with plastic wrap. Bloom the gelatin in ice water, squeeze it dry- then add it to warmed strained stock. Allow to dissolve. Add vinegar, diced shallots, salt and pepper to taste. Pour 1/8 inch of stock into the plastic lined terrine. Layer the chicken (about one quarter of the total meat) in to the stock. Then add a thick layer of parsley chiffonade. Continue to layer the meat and parsley with stock until all of the chicken and parsley is used up. You may have a bit of remaining stock. Wrap with plastic wrap and chill until firm, preferably overnight.
Slice in about 1 inch slices and serve with Béarnaise sauce.

Béarnaise Sauce:
3/4 cup unsalted butter (175g)
3 tbsp cider vinegar
3 tbsp dry white wine
3 shallots
1 tbsp tarragon, chopped
3 egg yolks
salt and espelette pepper to taste
1 tbsp chervil, chopped

Melt and cool the butter- boil the vinegar and wine with finely diced shallots, until reduced to one tablespoon. Add one tablespoon of water to cool the mixture. Add the egg yolks and seasoning, whisk briefly, then continue whisking over a bain marie for about 4 minutes. Take off the heat, whisk in the tepid butter little by little (like making aioli to form an emulsification) until the sauce thickens. Strain the sauce and stir in the herbs.

DESSERT:
HUNG YOGURT, HONEY, RASPBERRIES, PEACHES STUFFED WITH CRUMBLE

Ingredients:
Fresh ripe amazing summer Okanagan peaches ½ per guest
(or more!)
Ripe beautiful raspberries, about 1 pint for every 6 guests
Honey & honeycomb (honey to taste- they used about
1/8 cup for a pint of berries, about 1 tbsp sized chunk of
honeycomb is generous)
Approximately 2 tbsp of hung yogurt per guest

Crumble Ingredients:
(Joy Road served their dessert with chopped almonds
instead of crumble but Dana also supplied this recipe as an
option)
1 cup oats
1 cup unsalted butter, chilled
1 cup all purpose flour
1 cup almonds (John & Virginia have almond trees!)

THE WINEMAKERS/HOSTS:
Orofino Vineyards, Cawston

The 1.6 mile dinner is beautifully set behind Orofino's famous straw bale winery. The unique strawbale design has been around for over 200 years-the energy efficiency is unparalleled, naturally cool in our hot desert summer and retains heat well in the winter. Backdropped by dramatic mountainscape, 2012 marked the 5th year for this amazing concept dinner. Literally all of the ingredients served in the 1.6 mile dinner menu came from 1.6 miles around the winery. How do they know? Virginia drove around to each farmer the first year and basically measured the distance to the furthest one. It has evolved from the first event with 50 people in attendance, to two nights of 50 people plus a culinary farm tour, to the last version of 114 guests. The actual dinner is five courses long – Joy Road is sharing recipes for three courses of the delectable menu from 2012. All wines at the actual dinner were from Orofino's fabulous repertoire – we chose a neighbouring Similkameen winery's Chardonnay (Seven Stones) in place of the Orofino Chardonnay served with the dish to introduce another outstanding local winemaker.

In their own words:
"We came to the Similkameen at a time when we were looking for something new to try. Virginia had been nursing for quite a while and I was teaching at a small high school with a 40 minute commute one way. Life was pretty safe but we wanted to try something together and thought we would like to farm something. Virginia has a horticulture diploma with a specialty in greenhouse crop production, which led us to search for a place to start a greenhouse operation. My parents had retired to Kelowna and one day spotted a vineyard for sale. The rest is history.

We eat very well here and are lucky to share with some other families who love the same sort of thing. We'd like to eat more often together but work schedules get in the way like most everyone. The food isn't always fancy but it is always good and we all drink too much wine. Its fun. European food culture is like that too, I think. Traditional meals that linger for hours happen there as well but probably not as often as they would like.

Regarding change, I think the rules surrounding abattoirs are absurd. In this time of local food explosion, the rules surrounding meat production are prohibitive and playing into the hands of the big players. Its really not what the public wants. This has to change. The Similkameen is just a bit more off the radar. We kind off revel in being the undiscovered valley. The vibe is very laid back, slower than the Okanagan, and we tend to over-deliver on visitors expectations. Something like 90% of the farmers at the Penticton Farmers' Market are actually from here in Cawston. The wines are pretty terrific here too as our diverse terroir really seems to show through."

Oyster Festival

Kicking off the year, the 1st Annual Oyster Festival brought the ocean to the desert end of our valley. Walnut Beach Resort in Osoyoos put on an effing good shuck fest leaving slurpers giddy with all you can eat oysters paired with local wine and beer. Oyster farmers/celebrity shuckers came in from the Coast including Rob "Effing" Oyster from Effingham Oysters to compete in a shucking contest. Kelowna's celebrity Fishmonger Jon Crofts from Codfather's Seafood was key in this event as well as the Spot Prawn Festival and the fundraising efforts to help local Sockeye salmon return to our lakes. Local chefs wow'd with creative oyster bites and wine pairings on day 2 on the sunny patio at the Resort. All await the 2nd Annual with baited breath. (Especially Bill Eggert from Fairview Cellars in Oliver, who downed a record 52 raw oysters on day 1).

Mignonette
Jennifer Schell

A perfect pairing with a luscious raw oyster - this Mignonette features Okanagan bubbles and should be paired with same. Serve alongside a variety of BC shucked oysters with traditional tabasco and lemon wedges.

Ingredients:

1/4 cup Okanagan sparkling wine or frizzante
2 tbsp Okanagan white wine vinegar
1 tbsp shallot, minced
1 tbsp chives, chopped
pinch of salt and a dash of fresh cracked pepper

Whisk together first three ingredients and then stir in chives.

L-R - Kathy McLaggan, Jon Crofts & Rob ("Effing") Oyster Tryon before their shuck off.

193

Soup Sisters   **Broth Brothers**

Warming hearts...one bowl at a time

One of my great joys the last couple of years has been my involvement with Soup Sisters/Broth Brothers. An extraordinary organization, founded by one of my heroes, Sharon Hapton, in Calgary in 2009, it brings community together to create nurturing soup for local women and children in need. The concept is simple. Soup Sisters/Broth Brothers are year-round programs where participants pay a $50 registration fee to participate in a soup-making event at a local professional kitchen under the guidance of a chef facilitator. At our Kelowna chapter, my volunteer partners (Kalayra Angelyys, Heather Schroeter, Avery Trent) and I organize groups of people each month at our "soup kitchen." Okanagan Street Food Restaurant, under the caring direction of owner Chef Neil Schroeter, and us make soup for the Kelowna Women's Shelter. Each month we create a one month supply (approx 60L) of soup that is ladled into individual covered glass bowls and 1L containers, labeled with names, ingredients and soup making team names, and then delivered to the Shelter's freezer.

Since March of 2009, over 60,000 containers of soup have been delivered to shelters from East to West, and there is a growing network of over 5500 Soup Sisters and Broth Brothers participants across the country. www.soupsisters.org

- Jennifer Schell

okanagan
street food
market *and* catering
www.okanaganstreetfood.com

THE CHEF

Neil Schroeter, Okanagan Street Food

Chef Neil Schroeter is a local pioneer in the street food truck world. His Okanagan Street Food truck was a destination for many when parked at the Kelowna Farmer's Market. Also a sought after caterer, the opening of his Okanagan Street Food Restaurant – open for breakfast and lunch- was a dream come true for fans. He and wife Heather Schroeter, General Manager at Kelowna's Manteo Resort are very involved in the local community.

In his own words:
"Growing up we spent many summers in the Okanagan, my family was from Osoyoos and my Grandparents still live there. I always loved the valley and when my parents retired to Vernon we decided to move here. I think the food style here has become more casual and less pretentious, good quality ingredients are more important than ever. The influx of hospitality industry professionals and foodies drawn by the lifestyle and weather gives great diversity to the valley both in food styles and support of unique restaurants. After 7 years as Chef at Sumac Ridge Estate Winery's Cellar Door Bistro I needed a change. I wanted to sell fresh food at the local farmer's markets. I had almost all my restaurant menu available from the truck, plus retail fresh pastas, pasta sauce, soups, stocks and house made crackers.
I did five markets a week for three years before we opened the restaurant but still have the truck for catering and events."

Heirloom tomato gazpacho w/ lemongrass poached prawns

Chef: Neil Schroeter, Okanagan Street Food Restaurant & Catering
Soup Sisters/Broth Brothers, Kelowna

Serves 6 as an appetizer, 4 as a light meal.

Chilled Soup:
2 lbs heirloom tomatoes washed and cored (5-6 large)
1 medium English cucumber, washed
1 red pepper, washed and seeded
1 yellow pepper, washed and seeded
1 small jalapeño pepper, washed and seeded (optional)
½ small onion, peeled and diced
1-2 cloves garlic, peeled and minced
4 cups tomato juice
1 tsp Worcestershire sauce
3 dashes pepper sauce
kosher salt and freshly ground black pepper to taste

Rough chop all vegetables, mix with remaining ingredients in a tall container or jug. Purée with stick blender (leave it a little chunky).
Adjust taste with salt and pepper. Cover and chill overnight to let flavours develop (prepare up to 2 days in advance). Note: garlic and onion flavors will intensify - go easy.

Lemongrass Poached Prawns:
1 lb 21-25 prawns peeled, de-veined, rinsed in cold water and drained
1 small onion finely diced
1 medium carrot finely diced
1 stalk lemon grass outer stalk removed and roughly chopped
1 tsp canola or grape seed oil
1 tsp pickling spice
1 tbsp tom yum soup paste (hot and sour soup paste)
1 lemon zested and juiced
1 tbsp fresh ginger peeled and minced
3 cups water or vegetable stock
1/4 cup white wine
1 small bunch cilantro
1 pinch freshly ground black pepper

Sauté onion, carrot and lemongrass in oil over medium heat 4-5 minutes, add pickling spice, lemon zest and black pepper cook 2 more minutes.
Add all ingredients except cilantro and prawns and bring to boil, reduce heat and simmer 15 minutes. Bring back to boil and remove from heat, add prawns and cilantro stir until prawns are orange outside and opaque throughout. Let cool in liquid and chill overnight.

Quick Crème Fraiche:
1 cup whip cream
1 tbsp sour cream

Mix together and let sit on the counter overnight at about 20ºC until thickened, season with salt and pepper and chill in fridge until ready for use.

To plate:
Chill soup plates or bowls in fridge, ladle soup into bowls, drizzle or dollop crème fraiche over soup, garnish with prawns and more chopped cilantro.